PRAISE FOR 'H' JOHN MEJIA
AND HIS NEW BOOK
Step Into Your Zone

"I knew the moment I heard H's voice that there was something special about him, but I had no idea he would be the one who changed the trajectory of my television career.

"After a successful, fifteen-year career as broadcast TV news anchor, I was ready to embark on a new adventure, which would take me from Minneapolis, MN, to Tampa, FL. I was making my rounds, cold calling prospective job opportunities, when I dialed the number I found on his *Good Life Tampa Bay* TV show website. Every other person I talked to didn't have time to learn my name, let alone the experience and hard work ethic I was ready to offer, but 'H', with his curiosity and kindness, listened, inquired, and learned about me. It was a ten-minute phone call, but in those ten minutes, he heard something that he knew could benefit the both of us.

"That is 'H'. He doesn't just stay status quo; he is constantly looking for ways to build his business, himself, and, something you don't see very often these days, build others up as well. In our decade-long friendship, 'H' has shown me just how far hard work, perseverance and kindness can take you. Over the years, he shared his 'playbook secrets' with me, and it's something I will be forever grateful for. Readers can now benefit and learn them too, from his new book *Step Into Your Zone*."

—Rebekah Wood, Television Personality,
On Air National Television Host,
Award Winning Broadcast TV News Anchor

"What's up 'H', to another Bayside Commodore alum. Listen, I know your name is 'H', but I like the John part, like Daymond John, anyway. We have so much in common; I know we grew up in a great area and it made us who we are. We also knew that growing up, we had to change the world. I know you are trying to get more people to become focused in these crazy times. Congratulations on your new book, *Step Into Your Zone*. I know my buddy and fellow Shark, Kevin Harrington, wrote the Foreword. See, now you have two sharks right now – and I'm sure you'll get 10 sharks endorsing you, because you're a shark as well. Congratulations on everything and keep trying to change lives and get people excited about stepping into their zone. All the best! I look forward to seeing you, and thank you for educating and empowering people."

—Daymond John, Entrepreneur
Shark from *Shark Tank* TV Show
Founder, President, and CEO of FUBU

"As a former college basketball player, I know what 'The Zone' is all about and what it takes to get there. Like 'H,' I have transferred those same principles from sports into my business career in building a national company as the Co-Founder & President of College HUNKS Hauling Junk & Moving Company, the largest and fastest growing junk removal and moving franchise opportunity in North America. One of our company's core values is to build leaders and we make it a point to inspire every team member, so that we can all reach our maximum potential and achieve greatness. Every day, our entire team works hard to strive and achieve 'The Zone' in taking care of our customers! I have known 'H' over the last eleven years and have been interviewed by him numerous times on his *Good Life Tampa Bay* TV show as he has done stories about the dynamic growth we have experienced as a company. In addition, I have also appeared as his feature story on his one-hour *Business Zone* TV Show. 'H' is a true professional and is passionate about the work that he does. I have always had great experiences on my TV interviews with him. Yeah, the guy is in 'The Zone' with what he does. His new book, *Step Into Your Zone*, will give you the foundation of principles and tips to help you elevate your game to the next level."

—Nick Friedman, Co-Founder & President,
College HUNKS Hauling Junk & Moving Company,
(Annual Revenues 100 million + and Over 100 franchises nationwide)

"I've known 'H' for over forty years. From the time we both entered college through today, he's always displayed great passion and discipline to have success. His book *Step Into Your Zone* is about the things you need to do in your life to succeed in business, or everyday life. Many of the principles and lessons you will read about, I've used myself, and they helped me play twenty-two years in the NFL. A must-read book!"

—Sean Landeta, Former NFL Punter (1985–2006),
Two-time Super Bowl Champ,
Six-time All Pro

"For a number of years, I had worked with 'H' John Mejia as a co-host on a TV show he hosted and produced on Fox Sports for the Playboy Celebrity Golf Tournament in LA. He is a true professional! I have seen firsthand how well he coordinated every aspect of production, from the show script to handling the production crew and talent, and ultimately producing a great one-hour TV special. Working with celebrities, professional athletes, and corporate executives in a demanding four-day event is not an easy task. Lots of personalities to deal with. He was always a delight to work with! I know his book can give you the tips that can help you achieve more!"

—Brande Roderick, Actress & Model,
Starred in television shows like *Celebrity Apprentice* and *Baywatch Hawaii*; her movie career includes *Starsky & Hutch*, *Dracula II*, and *The Nanny Diaries*. Former Playboy Playmate of the Year, and the author of *Bounce, Don't Break*. She is the founder of several companies and her newest venture is with Alkaline88 water and selling luxury homes as a celebrity realtor in Southern California.

'H', what's up buddy? I want to congratulate you on your new book. You know you had that Fox Sports Playboy Golf Show, where you interviewed me several times. You're a great guy and we had a lot fun, and a big shout out to you Mr. 'H'. I hope the book is a big success, like my books *Juiced* and *Vindicated* was. Again buddy, all the success and all the best! Take care."

—Jose Canseco, MLB Player
Power Hitter, Author and Baseball Commentator

"There is another level of Superior Performance that you should be living at in Life & Business! In order to get there, you must be willing to step all the way into your zone! There is a zone created just for you that 'H' John Mejia is about to guide you into. For over seventeen years, I have gleaned best practices from 'H'. My brand has grown exponentially because of his commitment to excellence. 'H' only surrounds himself with THE BEST, and in this book you're gonna learn what it takes to become THE BEST in your industry and in your life. 'H' and I have done it all. From Sizzle Reels and Convention Center stages to Business Reality Television. If you're ready to live your life to the fullest, STEP all the way in, with 'H' John Mejia's new book *Step Into Your Zone!*"

—Delatorro L. McNeal, II, MS, CSP,
CEO & Chairman of Platinum Performance Global, LLC,
Peak Performance Expert, Global Keynote Speaker, Best Selling Author and
Executive Producer

"I met 'H' John Mejia thirty years ago, and immediately felt his superstar presence—he's a big guy with a huge smile and bright eyes, dressed to impress, and a ball of enthusiasm. I hired him on the spot as a salesman. He was immediately the top rep in the company and I was so impressed with his ability to be "in the zone"—laser focused and a great listener with an easy and instant bond with almost anyone; a rare combination of polished yet relatable. There were times when I knew 'H' was exhausted, but I can guarantee you he never had a meeting where the person across the table ever sensed it. When he steps into the arena, any arena, it is game time, no matter what else is going on outside that arena or how he felt the minute prior. He is so genuinely interested in each person he interacts with that he both gains and gives energy instantaneously. He very quickly blossomed from star salesperson to star manager where he proved to be a tremendous sales trainer and motivator and was able to teach people his own highly developed methodologies. I had the pleasure of watching as 'H' became a business leader and an entrepreneur. At the same time, he learned to bring his 'in the zone' approach into every aspect of his life, and to no surprise, they have helped him become a fantastic dad and husband. His positivity and infectious enthusiasm light up a room and make him an absolute joy to spend time with. I know this book will leave readers better equipped to squeeze the most out of every opportunity in sales, business and life."

—Ken Mann, Managing Director,
SC&H Capital

"Hey, 'H', what's up man? It's been a long, long time since our interview, been many years since our Fox Sports interview. I wanted to say congratulations on your new business book, *Step Into Your Zone*. Anybody that's looking for a good book to read, check out *Step Into Your Zone*. Good luck!

—Terrell Owens, NFL Player
NFL Hall of Fame - WR

"I have gotten to know 'H' John Mejia over the last ten years. He has been not only someone that we do business with, but also a real inspiration to our team with his cutting-edge strategies to help us grow sales. Just reading the first few pages of his book shows what a genuine person he is and being able to remember all the people that have impacted his life. That speaks volumes to how many people he has befriended in his professional career. 'H' always has a great sense of calm and always listens first to understand other people's needs. That has taught me a lot (if I could only emulate that!). This book has many of the strategies he has shared with my team over the years to help us increase sales revenue and customer loyalty. I know it can do the same for readers!"

—Brad Resch, President,
Gulfeagle Supply (National Roofing Company in over 70 cities in the US)

"What's up 'H'. Hey man, I just want to wish you well on your upcoming book, *Step Into Your Zone*. I hope that it's a success, and I look forward to working with you more after the Covid-19 pandemic is over. God bless you, and I wish you all the success in the world. God bless you, 'H'."

—Derrick Brooks, NFL Player
NFL Hall of Fame - LB

"'H' John Mejia has such a positive impactful presence about him. We are so blessed that he took interest in our humanitarian work and has captured it and the heart and growth of our jewelry company over the years. We have gone from eight to seventy employees and have become one of the most successful family-owned jewelry companies in the United States. 'H' is an incredible businessman and visionary person. His ability to tell our story has certainly had a huge impact of how we have been embraced by our community. I would think anyone would want to read his recipe for success! We think the world is a better place with him in it and people should hear what he has to share in his new book *Step Into Your Zone*."

—Steve and Julie Weintraub,
Owners of the Gold and Diamond Source and Founders of Julie Weintraub's
Hands Across the Bay Charity

"I had the pleasure of coaching 'H' during his college football career. 'H' has always been a leader and highly competitive possessing a great work ethic. His attitude has always been 'Why settle for second place if first is available.' In his senior year, he co-captained our team to an ECAC Lambert Cup Championship, a #4 National Ranking, and a National Playoff Appearance. Regardless of the venue, everybody today is looking for the edge. His book is filled with inspiring thoughts that will equip you, if embraced, to compete in the "ZONE."

—Phil Albert, Former Head Football Coach,
Towson University (1969–1991)—5× 'Coach of the Year'
& San Diego Chargers NFL—Game Day Scout (1994-2001)

"Oh my goodness, I'm not going tell anybody how many years we go back; we go way back. I am not going disclose even what project we met on. But I just want to say congratulations on your new book, that's amazing, *Step Into Your Zone*. Congratulations! I can't wait to get my hands on it and share it with everybody. That is amazing, and what an accomplishment. Want to wish you the best of luck, sending you beautiful, positive energy. Great to hear from you. You're crushing it. Keep it up, 'H'!"

—Brooke Burke, TV Host and Personality
Actress, Model, and Dancer

"I worked with 'H' when he was just beginning his media career and learning the craft. Though it was over twenty years ago, I still remember the intensity he brought to the gig. Always wanting to do that 'one extra take' on a stand-up or voice over so that he would be satisfied with his efforts! Having read *Step Into Your Zone*, I realize that I was in my 'Zone' during those days, and I'm now incentivized to recapture that spirit once again. Thanks for the reminder, 'H'!"

—Rick Boyer, Television Producer,
Cincinnati on the Go TV Show

"After graduating from college with a marketing degree, I found myself in the ever so 'sexy' electrical industry. I was eager to bring some new marketing strategies and opportunities to my customers. Then I was introduced to 'H.' While it has been over twenty years since we first met, 'H' still amazes me to this day. We had instantly connected over having the same Alma Mater. Then I saw the full package. 'H' is dynamic, passionate, honest, intelligent, and forward thinking. Oh, did I mention energetic???? That is an understatement! No matter what challenge is in front of him, he remains positive and steadfast in resolving the issue at hand. Most importantly, he approaches life with humor and has all the qualities you want in a friend and businessman. 'H' lives his life in the 'Zone.' I have come to look up to him as a mentor and leader and strive to be self-aware of those same leadership qualities within myself. His book helps to remind all of us how to be the best we can be!"

—Kelly Koch, Director of Marketing Programs,
IMARK Group (900 plus companies with 26 Billion + in Annual Sales)

"I know your nickname is 'H' but we never knew what 'H' stands for. Anyway, you used to interview me way back in the day at the Playboy Celebrity Golf Tournaments. Man, congratulations on your new book, *Step Into Your Zone*. You always made it real easy on me doing interviews, so I appreciated that. Anyway, just wanted to say congratulations, 'H'. Have a good one!"

—Eric Dickerson, NFL Player
NFL Hall of Fame - RB

"It's about time 'H' wrote this book. His wisdom, leadership, and coaching shine through. Talk about being in a zone, 'H' has been working toward this book for his entire adult life. Incrementally, he has been building momentum, acquiring skills, proving theories, and demonstrating results year over year. His ability to stay focused and in his zone has culminated in this 'must read' book. This is the road to real magic. Follow his path and soon, you will see the impossible become possible. In fact, the endorphins that fire from each success will lead you to looking for 'what's next.' Success doesn't just happen—it is a quest; it is an evolution—it is intentional. When you know what you are doing and you choose to take the right steps, success compounds. With sharp focus and a mentor like 'H,' you will soon find yourself with a gift as you *Step Into Your Zone*. Thank you for sharing your passion and your insight."

—Brad Callahan, Entrepreneur,
Travel and Hospitality

"Hi 'H', Jim Leyritz, from the NY Yankees, and I hope all is going well. I just want to congratulate you on your new business book, *Step Into Your Zone*. You always did a great job on our interviews on Fox Sports. Again, I want to wish you the best of luck, 'H'. You take care, and God bless."

—Jim Leyritz, MLB Player
NY Yankees

"I have had the extreme pleasure of working with 'H' on two occasions. In both cases, he overwhelmed me with his creativity, his professionalism, and his willingness to go the extra mile. He is a man of deep character, commitment to service, and amazing talent. He truly practices being 'in the zone' in every aspect of his life and work. I highly recommend him to anyone who wants to grow their business and enhance their lives. I also love his book—I read half the book in one sitting the moment I opened the manuscript… and I am not even a football fan! It is clear, practical, and filled with relevant stories from H's former football career. It challenged me to examine those times in my life when I have been 'in the zone' to experience that euphoric state even more in my life and work. I highly recommend it to anyone who wants to achieve peak performance in all aspects of their lives."

—Barbara Glanz, Hall of Fame Speaker,
Author of *The Simple Truths of Service* with Ken Blanchard and *CARE Packages for the Workplace*

"I first met 'H' after my time performing on *The Voice*, the TV show on (NBC). He interviewed me about my life changing experience. He was very professional and has this great way of keeping the energy flowing. It's very refreshing having someone effortlessly bring out your best qualities in a TV interview. Made me totally comfortable. I'm grateful to have had the experience with 'H.' The guy was in the ZONE and he helped me get in the zone with him during our thirty-minute TV interview together. His new book, *Step Into Your Zone*, will help you with secrets to get you there too!"

—R. Anthony—Recording Artist / Singer,
Singer on Season 3 of the hit NBC-TV show, *The Voice*
Performed in front of a 15 million TV viewing audience and in front of the four celebrity judges: Christina Aguilera, Blake Shelton, Adam Levine, and CeeLo.

"Hey, 'H' what's up, man? Joey Fatone here. Congrats on your new business book, *Step Into Your Zone*. Good luck, and of course you always do a good interview. Not too bad. I'm not gonna lie, you do pretty good. I hope it's a best seller! Much love and congratulations. Good luck, brother!"

—Joey Fatone, TV Personality
Singer, Dancer, and Actor
NSYNC

"TO ME HE WAS ALWAYS THE Big 'H'

"One of the biggest joys of coaching young men is to see them develop and become successful as players, husbands, fathers, and leaders. I had the pleasure of coaching 'H' at Towson State University. During those years, our program developed into an NCAA Division II power because of players like 'H.' Players with talent, integrity, enthusiasm, and love for their teammates.

"'H' played tight end for the Tigers, and was instrumental in our team's growing success. He could block, run precise routes, and catch the football as well as any of our skill players. He played with finesse, as many of our routes required reading the secondary coverage and finding a soft spot in zone coverage, and was equally effective at using strength to beat man coverage. 'H' practiced hard to develop his skills and was an example to players and coaches alike.

"His determination was never more evident than in his sophomore year when he developed a life-threatening viral cardiomyopathy, and was sidelined for an entire year. As he improved you could always find 'H' at practice keeping his head in the mental game. Once he was cleared to come back on the field, he continued to develop as a player and team leader. The trials and successes at Towson made you believe that 'H' was destined for something special.

"I've had a chance to review his new book, *Step Into Your Zone: Playbook of Secrets for Peak Performance in Business, Sales, and Life*, and believe it is an epistle for the young and the old, for men and women, and a detailed roadmap for success in any area of life. Anyone who reads it, and applies its principles, will be enriched."

"To the well-trod genre of Peak Performance, 'H' John Mejia delivers an insightful and approachable philosophy in *Step Into Your Zone*. His 'secrets' challenge popular myths (multitasking) and apply equally well to business, athletics, and personal connections. I've had the pleasure of working with 'H,' and know him to be a man of character and effectiveness. His zone clearly works for him and now he shares the process with the rest of us."

"The Big 'H', how are you man? God, it's been quite a while. The Big 'H', I haven't seen you in so long; I miss you. We had a good time at Hugh Hefner's Playboy Celebrity Golf Event. I heard about your new book, *Step Into Your Zone*. Congrats, brother! Congrats. I hear it's fantastic. I wish you good luck. Hope to see you soon. Peace and love, Big 'H'."

"'H' is the brother I never had. As teammates on the Towson University Football team, we formed a bond that remains cemented today. 'H' was the team captain and showcased his positive energy and motivation through his leadership. During a game against the University of Delaware, I had my nose severely broken. The team doctor and head trainer advised that I not play the remainder of the game. It was 'H' who came to the bench and asked me if I wanted to win this game. My answer was 'yes,' he said "We need you; push through this." Again, it was his motivation that lifted my desire to continue. We won that day. Our friendship has also secured a wonderful business partnership. 'H' has been an integral part of my business by designing and implementing promotional marketing programs for a global beverage company that drive execution and results. We can all gain tremendous insight on creating a powerful business mindset and using his cutting-edge strategies for top results in business and life. His book, *Step Into Your Zone*, is truly a playbook to results!"

—Mike Lewns #14
Former Teammate—Towson University Football WR,
National Beverage Co. Brand Director

"Working with 'H' was one of the most rewarding experiences when we combined our efforts to produce multiple shows (TV and highlight reels). As the former founder, President & CEO of Playboy Golf (a partnership and officially licensed entity of Playboy Enterprises), we were constantly facing unique situations that required a production/marketing company that could present our brand, our parent company's brand and our sponsors' brands at the highest level. He and his production team provided seamless start to finish footage without having to spend mega-hours in review. Working with Hollywood celebrities, professional athletes, and many of the most talented and beautiful models constantly provided challenges that 'H' was able to take on and create outstanding footage that the celebrities themselves couldn't wait to see. We always looked forward to seeing what 'H' created, and I wouldn't want to work with anyone else. Don't lose the opportunity to work with him; you'll give yourself a pat on the back for doing it! His new book, *Step Into Your Zone*, will give you the key ingredients, to help drive your next level success."

—Ajay Pathak
Former President & CEO, Playboy Golf

"I can write a book on the special qualities of 'H' John Mejia. Our bond and friendship started back in high school playing football together in NYC, in the borough of Queens. As a teammate, 'H' had the unique package of talents, from size, speed, and athleticism, to the great ability to catch a football. What impressed me most was his level of commitment to training, working out, preparation, and his intense drive to consistently improve. I remember during the summers—he and I would train and run pass plays on the field at 7 am and then at 6 pm after summer day jobs. He always went all out and pushed himself as hard as he could. Always a 100% committed work ethic. In our business careers, I have worked with 'H' and have implemented his media marketing strategies to help build the restaurants that I have owned in the NYC area. He always brought that same work ethic to business as well. As a close friend, I have witnessed 'H' over the years go through times of challenging struggles. I have also seen him make adjustments to work through those challenges and be resilient in turning things around. I know his book, *Step Into Your Zone*, will provide readers the playbook to guide them with the secrets to improve their game in business and life!"

—Joe DiGirolomo #19,
Former teammate Bayside HS Football QB,
Restaurant Entrepreneur

'H', this really takes me back, Playboy Golf Fox Sports. Great times. I remember your skits with NFL players and the one with Terrell Suggs. Oh my God! And The Best Damn Sports Show Period! That was a great show! I want to say, 'H', congrats on the new business book, *Step Into Your Zone*. Good luck with your book! Good luck to you, brother!

—Tom Arnold, Actor and Comedian
Movies included: *True Lies*, *Nine Months*, and *McHale's Navy*

"I am reminded with each interaction with 'H' John Mejia of his very special gifts. His unbridled, genuine enthusiasm, his passion. How he views any setback as an opportunity to grow, to learn, and how he has manifested that approach throughout his life. His genuineness, integrity, and deep, heartfelt compassion. All traits evident to me since we were both in grade school. A terrific person, a cherished friend, and an incredible mentor. His book, *Step Into Your Zone*, is terrific and challenges all of us to grow, expand, and get better in all areas of our life."

—Guy McNeil,
Corporate Executive, Industry Consultant

"Hi 'H' – congratulations on your new book, *Step Into Your Zone*, that is simply fabulous. Everybody needs to read a book on business. We all need that book on self-help. By the way, thank you for interviewing me through the years. Now I want to interview you on my show too. Everybody needs to get a copy of *Step Into Your Zone*. Thank you 'H'. Love you!"

—Rhonda Shear, TV Personality
Comedian, Actress, and Entrepreneur
TV Host of *USA Up All Night*
RhondaShearSocialHour.com

"Over the years, 'H' was always the best to work with in helping us build our Celebrity Golf brand nationally. He and his production team were awesome working with our celebrities, pro-athletes, the competing golfers, and corporate sponsors. He was brilliant in producing TV shows over a nine-year period. 'H' is special and his new book will give you the instructions you need to create the results you want in business and life!"

—John Pulitano,
VP, Tournament Celebrity Golf Director

'H', great interviewing with you at Lou Piniella's Celebrity Golf classic event, and congratulations on your new business book, *Step Into Your Zone*. I wish you all the best with that, and I can't wait to get my copy!"

—Antonio Tarver, Pro Boxer
Former Boxing Champion
Actor in *Rocky Balboa*
Boxing Analyst Showtime

"*Step Into Your Zone* is a book about our struggle to achieve the absence of doubt, comparison, and most importantly, the absence of self-judgment. 'H's' stories and examples are fresh reminders that anyone, who chooses to believe, can define their space and place in this world."

—Victor Antonio, International Sales Trainer, Speaker, and Author,
Sales Velocity Academy

"'H' John Mejia does everything with passion and with the highest level of integrity. With his wonderful marketing mind, methodical preparation, and relentless work ethics, projects come to completion stress free and on time. I've had the distinct privilege to work with 'H' on several projects since 2013 and working with him always provides for a wonderful, life-enriching experience. His new book reveals the secret combination to unlock the success you are working toward."

—Bobby D., Entrepreneur,
On-Line Show Producer

"I have worked with 'H' over the years on various marketing initiatives, and he has always delivered above and beyond. Spending time with 'H' is energizing! I always leave our conversations ready to make a difference in my day! He is always in the zone. His new book will give you the information you need to know how as well."

—John Russ, Marketing Director,
Wholesale Distributor

"'H' has been an amazing partner for my video productions over the last few years. I say 'partner' because he and his team have a vested interest in your vision and take the time to brainstorm with you to ensure you vision is fulfilled. 'H' and his production team are the consummate professionals and have always operated within the 'zone' with me. If you want a solid playbook to not only get you in your Zone, but also continuously succeed at the top of your 'zone,' you need H's new book."

—Kelly Charles-Collins, Esq., MBA
Attorney, TEDx Speaker, Author
CEO, HR Legally Speaking, LLC

"'H' and I go way back as college football teammates. We connected right away because we were both from the NYC area. As teammates, I saw 'H' do the little things right to be able to play at a high level and be in the Zone on the field. Years later, in our business careers, I hired 'H' to create a customer loyalty program for my division to get a competitive edge in the market. 'H' delivered. He's a great friend and his new book is a must read if you want to elevate your business game and find that Zone, while learning how to deal with challenging times!"

—Joe Varello, College Teammate,
Corporate Executive,
Fortune 100 Company

"I have worked in the corporate incentive marketing arena with 'H' for 19 years. During that time, I have witnessed his special talents and mind set. From his preparation, ability to deliver dynamic presentations, and his focused determination on providing clients cutting edge solutions that deliver positive ROI. 'H' consistently plays the corporate world in the 'Zone'. His book, *Step Into Your Zone*, will give those who desire, a fresh perspective on upping their business game too."

—Dan Cross, Business Development Team
Corporate Executive
Incentive Marketing

"Hey 'H', it's been a long time since that interview with me, you, and Seth Joyner. What a great time that was. Listen, I just want to say congratulations on your new book, *Step Into Your Zone*. What a great name for a book and I look forward to reading it. I know it's going to be a best seller. Hang in there."

—Lawrence Taylor ('LT'), NFL Player
NFL Hall of Fame- LB

"*Step Into Your Zone* is the ultimate playbook for how to succeed in business and in life. 'H' John Mejia has done a wonderful job putting together a map that draws from his wisdom and experiences in both business and sports. The most compelling thing about is 'H' is the real deal. An accomplished collegiate athlete as an All-American Tight End and outstanding success in the business world. Great read!"

—Jamie Peterson, College Teammate,
Corporate Executive Medical Field

Step Into Your ZONE

*Playbook of Secrets for
Peak Performance in
Business, Sales, and Life*

Entrepreneur,

'H' JOHN MEJIA

Celebrity TV Host & Producer,
Media Marketing & Sales Strategist

ISBN 978-1-09833-761-2 eBook 978-1-09833-762-9

WITH ALL MY LIFE'S up and downs, there is a core group that is my inner circle of strength that I celebrate and dedicate this book to: my loving wife Xiao who keeps me grounded and always brings out the best in me; my two amazing daughters, Alexis and Sofia, who mean everything to me and have provided me life's greatest gift of being a dad; my stepson, Alex, who inspired me to be a decent second dad and who prepared me well for Alexis and Sofia; my parents, Hernando and Aira Mejia, who were always there to support and cheer me on, no matter what; and my two sisters (my homies from the beginning in Jamaica, Queens, NY), Veronika and Sintra!

ACKNOWLEDGEMENTS

There are so many people I need to thank in writing this book. I realize that my life has been an incredible journey filled with so many cool experiences. I have met so many interesting people who have had a positive impact on my life and in some way have helped shape me into the man I aspire to be. I'm still a work in progress and I'm not done as the best is yet to come.

While some of my interactions may have been brief, these people, as I reflect back, have had a lasting impact. I am grateful that our paths have crossed and there is a place in my heart of warm reflection.

Thank you to my family: grandparents, Adolf and Erna Balins, and Josephina Diaz Mejia; my uncles, Eduardo Mejia, Gonzalo Mejia, Ivan Mejia, Arturo Mejia, Mario Mejia, Janis Balins, Peter Balins, Victor Balins, and Aturs Timbra; my aunts, Marta, Vija, Enta Timbra, Ruth Jimenez Marquez, Jeannette Balins, and Anastasia Karas; my cousins, Vivian Timbra, Ritvars Timbra, Bobby Gribulis, Andra Gribulis, Maris Gribulis, Claudia Mejia, Ivan Dario Mejia, Bryan Buenaventura, Andris Balins, Juliana Balins, Melita Balestieri, Tom Guellert, Lisa Guellert Surdulescu, Sebaas Mejia, Maria Eugenia Mejia, and Hugo Janos; my nephews and nieces, Zach Misischia, Mike Misischia, Monica Sosa, and Amber Sosa;

Shout out to Spencer Teolis, and my bro-in-laws, Steve Misischia and Benny Karas.

Thank you to my NYC public school teachers: Ms. Douglas, Ms. Hans, Mr. Alper, and Mrs. Gruber.

I owe much to the many coaches who have helped me. Thank you to my Pop Warner football coaches from the Jamaica Raiders: Mr. T, Billy Cinderelly and Sean McCloskey. Thank you to my baseball coach, Al Austin. Thank you to my Bayside NY high school football coaches: Coach Harrison, Coach Nelson, Coach Schmidt, Coach Yacavone, and Mr. Pepe. Thank you to my Towson University college football coaches: Coach Phil Albert (best life teacher too), Coach Gordy Combs (always there during those tight times), Coach Rich Bader, Coach Jay Robinson, Coach Ron Head, Coach Terry Wanless, Coach Paul Buckmaster, Coach Mike Bennett, Coach Bryan Brouse, Coach Doc Stanley, Coach Fitz, and Trainer Terry O'Brien. Thank you to the Indianapolis Colts coaches Frank Kush, Mike Westhoff and to Player Personnel Bill Turpin. Thank you to Oakland Invaders coaches Fred Biletnikoff and Charlie Sumner.

I also owe a lot to the teammates whom I have shared the playing field with. Thank you to the Bayside HS Football Teams Players of 1976 through 1978, the Towson University Tigers Teams Players of 1979 through 1983, the 1984 Indianapolis Colts Players—especially Tim Sherwin and Pat Beach (I enjoyed my cup of coffee during my time there), the 1985 Oakland Invaders Players, and the 1989 and 1990 Harrisburg PA Patriots Players (Barry Cohen, it was nice to connect on the field with you one last time).

There are many good friends that I have made through the years, who have taught me a lot about friendship, life, and myself. Thank you to my childhood friend, Emanuel Brannon. Thank you to the Jamaica, Queens, NY, neighborhood boys, Glen Belekis, Rich McNeil, Guy McNeil, Manny, and Danny Barouty. Thank you to my Bayside high school football teammates: Joey DiGirolomo, Wally CasaNova, Bruce Baver, Ken Breuer, Jamie Covington, Jerry Gusick, Donald Roach, Ron DiGirolomo, Bob DiGirolomo, Chuck Smith, Anthony Foster, John Barounis, and Kevin Dyevich. Thank you to Mr. and Mrs. DiGirolomo, Joanne DiGirolomo, Tina DiGirolomo, and Robert Sullivan. Special thanks to Bob Breuer, Yvonne Breuer, and the entire Breuer Family during my high school years. Thank you to my college teammates: Rich Walker, Jamie Peterson, Mike Lewns, Joe Varello, Kevin Fidati, Ron Meehan, Ed Aleshire, Glenn Meyers, Tom Zink, Sean Landeta, Joe Anderson, Barry Cohen, Vaughn Harman, Mike Preston, and Bret Rogers. Thank you to my Tiger Football fellow co-captains: Gary Rubeling, Donny Washington, and Pat Murphy. Thank you to Nancy Amann, John Amann, Jan Amann, and the entire Amann family. Thank you also to Don Iodice, Don Bowers, and Julian Orlenski. Thanks to Pete Schlehr and Dan O'Connell the Sports Info Directors at Towson Univ. To the Sports Dept., Michele O'Connor, and Dan Crowley at Towson Univ. Thank you to the voice of the Tigers, Spiro Morekas.

I have been fortunate to have some amazing business partners through the years. Thank you to my fellow Towson University Tiger brother Tom Coffeen, Brain Bell, Nick DelCorso, Sam Toumayan and Greg Toumayan. Thank you, Brian Sawin and Ed Favara, who have been with me filming and editing on our TV production journey, of over two thousand hours of footage and interviews during our over-fifteen years and counting time capsule.

Thank you, Stephen Horn, Bryan Byrd, Daun Stipo, Dianna Babington, Brad Callahan, Ken Mann, Greg Daniels, Michael Stratti, Bernie Theriault, Kara Theriault, Mary Lee Theriault, Tom Theriault, John McMullin, Larry Bush, Sam Roy, Dan Cross, Steve Litzau, John Ebann, Jodi Nicholson, Denise Horton, Kevin Klimowski, Grant Riley, William Blair, Ajay Pathak, Tom Carmody, Donna Tavoso, John Pulitano, Rosanna Singer, Steve Ruane, Kelly Koch, Bob Smith, Bobby D, Bill Osborne, Rob

Haynie, Bridgette Bello, Alexis Muellner, Ian Anderson, Deanna Brooks, Kelly Charles-Collins, Lana Marie, Erica Cobb, Crystal Davis, Laura Lynn, David Araujo, Mitch Billings, Randy Drake, Chrissy Cihlar, Anthony Chicklowski, Bill Taylor, Sibyl West, Kurt Eide, Ed Favara, Brian Sawin, Rebekah Wood, Colette Meyer, Dave Keimig, Brian Kreindler, Terry Lazin, Delatorro McNeal, Greg Borsari, Van Earl Wright, Lisa Dergan, Brande Roderick, Dr. Joe and Elif Fitzgerald, Usman Ezad and Rick Boyer.

Special thanks to Steve and Julie Weintraub, who believed in me and my TV show at one of the lowest points of my business career and during my personal struggles twelve years ago. I had lost everything and was ready to start again. They supported my vision for my *Good Life Tampa Bay* TV show. During this journey, to watch and document what they have developed in their business and their "Hands Across the Bay Charity" has been amazing. They have uplifted the entire Tampa Bay community. I am forever grateful to you both.

To my writing editor, Debbie Viguié, thank you for going through a garage full of my written content, reviewing all my interviews and stories, and all the hours of meetings together and then organizing this and helping me bring this thirteen-year dream of a book to life with me! Thank you to my team at Book Baby Publishing, especially Alex and Damon, for all the guidance in coordinating all the printing, conversions, book formatting, and international distribution set up. Thank you to the team at Smith Publicity led by Marissa Eigenbrood and Kristi Hughes. Thank you to Laura Maddrey who took my vision for the book cover and photo album and made it a reality.

Thank you to those whose teachings have inspired me: Phil Albert, Brian Tracy, Anthony Robbins, Jim Rohn, Zig Ziglar, Og Mandino, Dr. Waitley, Jay Abraham, Joel Osteen, Grant Cardone, Gary Vaynerchuck, Darryl Strawberry, and Kevin Harrington. Special thank you to my two brothers from another mother, Victor Antonio and Delatorro McNeal, for your friendship wisdom, and business ventures.

Thank you to those who I did TV interviews with and used some of their wisdom and shared it in this book: Kevin Harrington, R Anthony, Nick Friedman, Darren Prince, Kato Kaelin, Rhonda Shear, and Darryl Strawberry.

Special thank you to those celebrities that I have interviewed over the years, and at my request, gave me a nice shout out through Cameo, they are: Antonio Tarver, Brande Roderick, Brian Dunkleman, Bridget Marquardt, Brooke Burke, Christian Okoye, Eric Dickerson, Derrick Brooks, Eric Dickerson, Gretchen Rossi, Jeremy Piven, Jim Leyritz, Joey Fatone, John O'Hurley, Jose Canseco, Kato Kaelin, Lonie Paxton, Ray Lewis, Rhonda Shear, Seth Joyner, Steven Bauer, Terrell Owens, Tia Carrere, Tom Arnold, Vinny 'Paz' Pazienza, Anthony Anderson, and Lawrence Taylor ('LT'). Big 'Shark' thank-you to Kevin Harrington and Daymond John.

I know there are so many more special people, that unintentionally, I have missed including. Regardless, you have impacted my heart on this life journey. Thank you.

Most importantly, I thank God as I am grateful and blessed by His love and forgiveness! The true and ultimate power and source through His Divine Spirit of Christ. For giving me the strength and insight to seek Him through it all, including my setbacks, challenges, and poor decisions. God's best is yet to come for all of us!

CONTENTS

FOREWORD

The Zone! I know it very well.

During my business career, as the creator of TV infomercials and being one of the Original Sharks on the hit TV show *Shark Tank* on ABC, I have experienced that high level of performance known as the "Zone" and I have worked with entrepreneurs and celebrities who consistently play and operate at that high level, too. In my opinion, getting to the "Zone" often and consistently is a prerequisite to achieving greatness in any endeavor.

Time and time again, I have witnessed the "Zone." Besides *Shark Tank*, as a global entrepreneur, I have personally reviewed thousands and thousands of business opportunities and pitches from inventors and deal makers. To generate the 500 products launches I have done, (while generating over 5 billion in product sales in over 100 countries), I have had to look at a lot of deals. You see, only a very small percentage of the deals I analyze get signed and launched. It's a numbers game for sure. The ones that make it through are definitely operating from the place known as the "Zone."

Being the "As Seen On TV" pioneer, I have built 20 businesses to over $100 million each. I'm known as the billion-dollar man because I can see the superstar talent and products that can deliver me "Zone" results. I have successfully brought products to the market such as Ginsu Knives, The Food Saver, The Great Wok of China and The Flying Lure. I have worked with amazing celebrities such as Tony Little, Billy Mays, George Foreman, Jack LaLanne, Hulk Hogan, Paula Abdul, Montel Williams, and the Kardashians. I've been featured on 20/20, CNN, Fox Business, Bloomberg, Jim Kramers the Street, MTV, *Good Morning America*, *The CBS Morning News*, *The Today Show*, *The View*, and even the *Daily Double* on Jeopardy! The common ingredient in all these great successes is that special place that top achievers operate and perform from, the place called, the "Zone."

I first met 'H' John Mejia years ago when he and his TV crew came to my launch party to do a story on one of my new projects. During my interview with "H," I immediately connected with him. He did a great job in his interviews with my team and me and produced a very nice story on us that aired on his *Good Life Tampa Bay* TV show. After seeing that story, I saw the very special talent that "H" had and suggested to him that he should do some infomercials for me. We did work on a few projects together and I can say from my experiences that "H" always goes all out, he is very talented, and always executes on what he promises. He is very thorough in his planning, has a great attitude, and guides people through great interviews with his warm and enthusiastic style. He consistently does all the little things right! He operates from the "Zone." His new book, *Step Into Your Zone*, will empower readers to look within themselves and use the lessons and principles that he shares to help them break through to that top level of performance known as the "Zone." A must-read book!

Kevin Harrington
Sent from a Shark
Inventor of the Infomercial
Best-Selling Author
Original Investor Shark on *Shark Tank*
www.kevinharrington.tv

PART I

WHAT IS THE ZONE AND WHY DO YOU WANT TO STEP INTO IT?

"It's always when you're pushed to the limit, challenged the most, and when you think you have no more to give. When you step into that resistance and keep pushing through your obstacles, that is where your growth occurs, and your abilities break through to the next level. That is where the realization of your higher-level talents come to fruition. That special place is called the Zone."

—'H' John Mejia

You might have heard athletes, businessmen, or creative types talk about the "Zone." They reference it when talking about something they did that was extraordinary or an effort or performance they gave that was truly great. They brought their A game. They left everything on the field. Their work or their performance was inspired. They are "in the Zone." The question is: what is the "Zone?"

Many scale the heights of greatness in pursuit of being the best, reaching peak performance, mountaintop experiences, Nirvana, and a dozen other names. Each and every one of them is looking to get into the

Zone. Very simply, the Zone is that place where you perform at your top level, and even better than that. You are able to go above and beyond and make incredible touchdown catches, accomplish Herculean tasks, or create something that is better than you thought yourself capable of. Top performers in every area (sports, business, and the arts) spend time in this place where everything comes together perfectly so that they can be at their best for a few seconds or a few hours. In the Zone, everything becomes clearer, easier, and you're able to maintain laser-like focus for as long as you need to. You get on a roll and things just start happening. It's like you cannot fail and everything is breaking your way.

I played high school and college football. (I was an All-American player.) I signed NFL, USFL, and MLFS free agent contracts with pro teams. Since then, I've been an entrepreneur who has been part of several multi-million dollar companies and have enjoyed a successful career in media and marketing as an award-winning TV host and producer, working with some of the biggest corporate brands, celebrities, and athletes.

I've faced a lot of struggles and setbacks, which I'll be discussing throughout this book. I've also had a lot of triumphs, game- and life-changing moments. As both an athlete and a businessman, I crave time spent in the Zone where I'm performing like it's my best day ever and everything falls into place.

Chances are you've been there at some point in your life. Have you ever been working on a project or closing a deal and all of a sudden everything just "clicked?" Maybe you were able to make connections or find solutions that had been eluding you or others. You could have even looked at the clock to discover that six hours had passed and you're not sure how because it doesn't feel that long. Perhaps you sat down to write that report, proposal, or game plan only to discover that instead of laboring over it, everything just came pouring out of you and onto the page with ease. Maybe you enjoy the challenging game of golf and found the Zone where every part of your game was on fire. From accurate long drives to finding the green with your wedge shot and then making that long birdie putt. (Oh, just an FYI, I have had very few Zone moments on the golf course.)

The Zone is a mental state you arrive at. When you're in it, you can feel it. You're unstoppable. Unfortunately, we can't live there all the time. With perseverance, though, we can return to that place. Top achievers in their fields hang around that peak far more often than others. You can train yourself to do that, too.

There is a great deal of personal satisfaction and joy that can come while you're in the Zone. There is also the added benefit of being able to accomplish a lot more at a lot higher consistency or quality over a short period of time. You want to be in the Zone for the experience itself. You also want to be there for the opportunity to achieve great things with far less effort than it would normally take. In this section we'll discuss what the Zone is, who it's for, and what it's like.

CHAPTER 1

What Does It Mean to Be at the Top of Your Game?

*The Zone is when you go above and beyond your personal best,
you transcend to a new level of performance and results!*

"Do your best." That's something we hear from the time we're little. Everyone around us wants to do our best and, ideally, we want that, too. The strange thing is, even when we do our best, the outcome isn't the same every time. Sometimes, things just seem to fall short. Other times, we're successful beyond what we normally are capable of. When you achieve the latter, it's called being in the Zone.

The Zone is a special place. As I mentioned, it goes by many traditional names including peak performance and Nirvana. It can also be defined as enlightenment, flow, and peak experience. Whatever label you want to give it, it's about that level of performance where you are absolutely at your best possible ability and even expanding above and beyond that ability.

I recently attended an alumni gathering with some of my teammates from my college football days. These were my brothers that I went to battle with at Towson State University (now known as Towson University). When we were playing together, we had some great experiences and great achievements, including the Lambert Cup Championship and making the NCAA National Championship Playoffs. I was a tight end. I caught passes, blocked, and made touchdowns.

I ended up talking with my former teammate Mike Lewns, who had been a wide receiver. I shared with him that when we would be playing there would be times when something weird would happen to me. I told him there'd be times when I would be running and then all of sudden it was like I was playing at a higher level and when I played at that higher level it almost had a dreamlike quality to it. It was as though I would see things in slow motion and I would cease being aware of the stadium, the fans, and the defensive coverage. I would be running effortlessly and I could hear my slow breathing really clearly. I'd look at the quarterback and it was almost like we locked eyes and were communicating silently. He'd throw the ball and I could see every freaking detail on that ball. I could see the tiny grain leather and the white laces of that ball. And I was so targeted and zoned in. I could even read the brand label on the football.

It's like the weirdest, most different place, and state of being. It's a feeling that I'm being challenged to do my best, but it's like complete perfection and everything feels easy. Any defender trying to distract me or grab the ball became non-existent even if they were all over me. They weren't part of my world because at that moment, it was just me and the football and I knew I was going to catch it. That's what we call the Zone. It's that experience, that moment. It's a slow-motion, dreamlike kind of place where great performances happen.

Once I finished describing my experiences to Mike, he said he knew exactly what I was talking about. There'd be times where he felt he made impossible catches, things that in all reality there should have been no way he could catch. Yet he did. That was because he was in the Zone. The Zone is when you go above and beyond your personal best—you're able to go to the highest level. Funny, we never talked about that as players; only years removed did we have that conversation and reflect back!

We're all familiar with Michael Jordan and Tiger Woods. We see great athletes at championship games, and you can just tell when they're in the Zone. They're killing it.

I experienced the Zone many times in football. Just as rewarding is when I've been able to experience it in my business career. I was able to take what I'd learned playing sports and transfer that into the business game. I've spent over two decades working with companies of all sizes, including Fortune 500 companies. I have done hundreds of TV interviews with business moguls, celebrities, and athletes and have been able to learn a lot about the Zone by being around them and speaking with them.

One of my Zone business experiences came with my client, Procter and Gamble, a company that does over 70 billion in annual revenue. I worked with them for a number of years, on a multi-million dollar promotional campaign, which I created for their Crest White Strip products. Originally, when the opportunity for Procter and Gamble came up, it came kind of easily. They were excited to talk to me and wanted me to follow up in two weeks. I hung up from the call confident that I had landed the contract. Only, when I called back in two weeks, it was a different story. The guy I had been talking with was just one member of a team that had to be convinced and other members of the team already had relationships with different agency vendors.

The guy told me, "I really don't know if you'll even want to come here. We've talked to four or five different companies already, other marketing incentive companies that have already been in here, companies we already know, and we've pretty much made our decision on who we want to go with."

I felt like I had just been punched in the gut. I had a decision to make on the spot. I could decide to give up because it sounded like they'd already made a decision and I didn't need to waste thousands of dollars in travel expenses. However, instantly, in my mind, I just felt that this was my account and I had an absolute clarity of vision about it. I told him I understood but I'd hate to see them have done all this work just to fumble the ball at the end zone. I explained to him exactly what it was I could offer that was unique and that it only made sense for them to hear what one of the leaders and innovators in the field could offer them. I was totally confident and committed in my delivery and recommendation.

He asked me to come in person for a meeting on Wednesday. I went and I owned that boardroom. Two weeks later, I signed the agency contract with them. My product didn't change, but my mindset, refusing to accept defeat and rising to the challenge, was what carried me through. If I hadn't been in the Zone on that phone call and again in the boardroom, I would have lost that deal. I was able to do that because I was mentally prepared and because I had the skills necessary to conquer the challenge ahead of me even if it meant stretching. That was one of the many fine moments in my business career where I was absolutely at the top of my game and operating in the Zone.

The Zone, that place where everything comes together and you excel, is available in sports and work. Whether you're an athlete, a businessman, or an artist, the Zone is the place you want and need to be.

CHAPTER 2

The Zone Is for Everyone

The Zone is available for everybody to have and experience. Membership is not exclusive!

Deep down, very few of us want to be mediocre. We want to be winners who achieve great things. Even if we don't have aspirations of being the very best in our prospective fields, we at least want to do our very best and live up to our own potential. Sure, there are a few people out there that don't have much interest in doing anything except skating by, but let's be honest, you're not one of those people or you wouldn't have even bothered reading this far. So, congratulations! You've already proven your desire and commitment to be and accomplish everything you can! Now, I'm going to help show you how to do that.

First of all, we need to get one thing straight. The Zone is not just for those who are the top 1% at what they're doing in comparison to the rest of the world. The Zone is not just for athletes. It's not just for those who have superior physical or mental skills. The Zone is a place that everyone can get to with dedication and hard work. It doesn't matter who you are, where you come from, how smart you are, how talented you are, how young or old you are, or what nationality, race, gender, or creed you are. Everyone can achieve peak performance in their chosen area of concentration.

The thing is—the Zone is a very personal experience. What peak performance looks like for you is different from what it will look like for anybody else, even those in the same profession. So, stop comparing yourself to other people. First of all, that's just a way to drive yourself crazy and make yourself miserable. Other people are just that—*other* people. You are not them anymore than they are you. You don't have the same backgrounds, life experiences, personalities, and everything else that makes each individual unique. Peak performance levels vary from individual to individual and that's a good thing! It's not like a test in school, where we're all being graded on the same thirty questions. It's a place of being, a state of mind, that is unique to you.

There are some similarities in everyone's experiences. For example, crystal clarity is an essential element of the Zone. It's one of the ways you know you've achieved that level. That doesn't mean everyone has clarity about the same thing or even experiences it in the exact same way. We all experience life through our own unique lens, our own perspective.

Whoever you are, whatever it is you do or want to do, the Zone is something you can achieve. Even better, the harder you work for it, the more effort you put in, the more often you can get there! Your success is not dependent on the success or failure of anyone else. While you may be in competition with other people in sporting events or sales incentives, you are only competing with yourself when it comes to achieving your own peak performance. The Zone is all about bettering your best!

CHAPTER 3

The Zone Is a Mental
and Physical State

*Life begins at the end of your comfort zone when you're pushed
to that limit. That's where growth and expansion happen.*

The Zone is both a mental and a physical state. Some of you might be tensing up right now thinking that you're not so good at the mental stuff or that you are seriously out of shape and don't ever see that changing. Don't panic! You don't have to be a genius and you don't have to be in good physical condition to get into the Zone. These two factors might limit just how much you can ultimately achieve, but not whether or not you can get there.

Now, to be clear, you're not going to be trying to achieve peak performance in an area outside of your expertise. The guy who is in poor shape and health is not going to be able to achieve peak performance in a football game simply because he has not conditioned body and mind to do so.

However, that same guy could easily get into the Zone when it comes to selling and closing six-figure deals if he has spent time learning to do that.

It takes a lot of mental preparation, including study, training, and repetition to prepare for the Zone. Several elements of the Zone require a certain level of mental discipline. These include laser focus, the ability to be in the moment, and self-confidence. We will be discussing these in more depth in the next section of this book.

It also often takes a lot of physical preparation to ready yourself so you can get into the Zone. Unless you're an athlete, this doesn't necessarily mean you have to worry about going and hitting the gym. Physical preparation covers a wide range of things, including getting comfortable speaking to others on the phone or in person in a sales situation. You might have the greatest product in the world, but if you aren't practiced in talking about it, you're not going to be able to get into the Zone and sell, sell, sell! You might try, but without the practice, the practical experience, you're going to come off as inexperienced, unsure, or worse to your audience. It doesn't matter if you're trying to sell to an audience of 1 or 1,000. You still need to be poised, have learned to speak clearly and be able to deliver a compelling and passionate presentation with absolute certainty.

It does also help, regardless of what you are doing, if you get proper sleep, exercise, and eat nutritional meals. These keep you sharp and focused whether you're pitching a baseball or an idea. It can also help your stamina, which is great because when you're actually in the Zone, in the moment, you want to stay there as long as you can to achieve as much as you can even if it's up to several hours.

Discipline over mind and body in some way are essential elements of getting in the Zone, being there, and staying there as long as you can. The Zone requires us to be thinking as clearly as we can and doing as much as we can to rehearse and practice everything so that when the time comes we don't have to think, we don't have to struggle, and we can just be in the flow.

TEN CHARACTERISTICS OF THE ZONE

Things Change When You Change.

Almost everyone has experienced being in the Zone at one time or another. While we may have been there and can recognize it when we are there, it can be hard to put into words what exactly it is and what happens when we achieve that level of peak performance.

There are ten basic characteristics of the Zone. These are the elements that you experience while in it but these are also largely the things you need to set your sights on and work toward if you want to achieve peak performance. In this section, we'll discuss each of those ten basic characteristics.

CHAPTER 4

Laser Focus

"It's the little details that are vital. Little things make the big things happen."
—*John Wooden (former UCLA Basketball*
Coach, 10 NCAA Championships)

Perhaps the most obvious and overriding characteristic of being in the Zone is complete absorption into what you're doing. You are laser-focused. It's like a beam of energy that is so strong that nothing can interfere with the power of that energy. Nothing exists for you but what you are focused on.

When I played football and I was in the Zone, I would be laser focused on catching the ball. Of course, I was always focused on doing that, but this kind of focus goes beyond what is normal. When it would happen, I couldn't hear anything because everything would be tuned out. All the stimulation of all the noise around would be defunct, wiped away. I was locked and loaded and there was just me and the ball. Nothing else mattered in that moment.

I'll give you an example. One particular play while I was in NFL training camp with the Indianapolis Colts required me to take an outside release and run the seam route while outrunning an LB who was covering me. As I gained the one step advantage, the QB at that time, Mike Pagel, released the ball to where I was running to. At the same time, there was another defender, the free safety, who started coming at me full speed and just as I caught the ball, totally unloaded a vicious hit on me. I had total laser focus on the ball and my objective. I caught the ball and held on after the hit. If at any moment during the play I had directed my attention to the impending collision, I would've lost focus on my objective of catching the ball. That's the type of focus required for the Zone.

A lot of experts have talked at length for years about the loss of our ability to focus as humans. We get distracted and pulled in a dozen different directions, often all at once, and it dilutes our concentration. That impacts our ability to remember things and to accomplish things.

Today, we have all this great technology that we love and use and the online social media platforms of communication. Things happen and are reported on a second to second basis. There's so much stimulation and distraction that people are getting lost, and they are getting pulled away from the things they should be doing and paying attention to. No matter what we do, we're constantly being overwhelmed with information and distractions. Everyone is vying for our attention. Advertisements from the radio, TV, and social media bombard us constantly.

A lot of people pride themselves on their ability to multitask. All multitasking means is that you've found a way to split your attention between a number of things so that you don't truly focus on any one of them to achieve excellence.

The other day I was driving on the highway. I was thinking of changing lanes so I looked over at the lane next to me. The woman driving the car next to me was putting on makeup while driving at a pretty decent speed.

Of course, my first thought was to jump on social media and tell my fans about it. I did not. But still, I was distracted by what was distracting her.

When we try to split our attention, it means that while we may show up to something, only part of us, about 20% is showing up. Let me tell you, 20% of your attention isn't going to help you get to the Zone. The Zone requires a 100% commitment to what you are doing in that moment.

You've got to be all in, you've got to show up, be there. It can't be a distracted or half-hearted effort. You ever been on the phone with a client or friend having a conversation while simultaneously texting someone else? You might think you're being efficient and saving time, but what you're actually doing is failing to give either of those people your best. If they are worth your time to communicate with at all, then they are worth your attention. And sure, you might churn through a decent list of tasks in a day, but you're never going to get to that place where you take your game to the next level and perform like a champion if you don't focus.

So, you need to retrain yourself. Learn to give yourself over completely to what you are doing. Learn how to let yourself be completely absorbed with one thing and it will give you a new understanding of the word "focus." Only when you learn to do that can you show up 100% and that is a critical prerequisite to getting to the Zone.

Imagine a baseball player trying to stand in the batter's box with one foot outside and then trying to hit a hundred mile-per-hour fastball. It's not happening. Same with a sales executive giving a multi-million dollar presentation, while checking their phone. Total focus and absorption are essential when they enter that stadium or boardroom if they ever hope at some point to get into the Zone.

So, start making a concerted effort to be 100% present for everything related to what you really want to do. If you're working, be fully there. If you're meeting with a client, give them all of your attention. If you're spending time with your family, stop checking up on work. It takes commitment and self-discipline to teach yourself to focus on what is in front of you, but without that you can't make it into your Zone.

"H" ZONE INTERVIEW ADVICE

from Kevin Harrington- Original Shark on Shark Tank TV show

"One of the very first books I bought was called *Think and Grow Rich* by Napoleon Hill. An unbelievable game changer. The whole concept of that was if you conceive it, and you believe it, you can achieve it. Those were the steps that Napoleon Hill said. Yep, you can get what you want in life. So, I have a saying now that whatever you 'vividly imagine, ardently desire, sincerely believe, and enthusiastically act upon, must inevitably come to pass'. And that is a quote by Paul J. Meyer from the SMI Institute. He's passed away now, but God bless him. I believe that the mind is so powerful that you can get what you want if you just set your sights [on] being a successful entrepreneur."
- Kevin Harrington

With over 500 products launched and generating over $5 billion in product sales in over 100 countries, Kevin Harrington is the inventor of the infomercial, As Seen on TV pioneer, and original shark on the Emmy award-winning TV show Shark Tank. For over 40 years, Kevin has built 20 businesses to over $100 million each. He is known as the billion dollar man.

CHAPTER 5

In the Moment

Be happy for this moment, this moment is your life.

So many of us are living our lives on autopilot. Have you ever had one of those days when five o'clock rolls around and you're hard-pressed to remember what exactly you did that morning? Even more on point, how often have you been heading to work or home and arrived at your destination with no real memory of actually driving there?

Being in the Zone is the total opposite. You're not thinking of the past or the future because you are 100% in the present and fully aware. Your action and your awareness of what you're doing becomes one. You are in the flow and you're creating that magic. It's like a dance. There's clarity of purpose, which brings total awareness, and nothing can make you deviate from that.

If you're playing football and you go out for a pass, you see your quarterback, you see the ball, and you and the ball are just part of the movement, part of the flow of action. It's going to reach you and you are going to catch it. The last play doesn't matter. The next play doesn't exist.

When you're in a sales presentation and you're in the Zone, you are fully connecting with your audience. You're not thinking about your next meeting or what you're going to have at lunch. You're not remembering that your spouse asked you to run some errands on the way home. All that exists is the here and now and the connection you have with your audience, as you give them the presentation. You are bringing your entire brain, your entire personality, your entire attention to the moment you're in and the people, and things that are there with you.

Our brains are constantly thinking, going a million miles an hour, and it can make it hard to be in the moment. We're thinking about what happened earlier in the day and we're anticipating what's going to be happening that night or over the weekend. You might smell someone's aftershave, and it's the kind your father used to wear, and it makes you miss him and think about the last time you saw him. The person on the other side of the door might be laughing, telling a joke to your coworkers and part of you is listening, wanting to hear what's so funny. You can hear the alert on your phone that you're getting texts, emails, phone calls. You have the urge to check.

You know you're supposed to be laser focused on the task at hand, but being in the moment takes it even a step deeper. You might be laser focused on the presentation you're giving but your mind could be racing ahead to the end of it, thinking about the 'ask' and how exactly you're going to phrase it. That's no good. You need to be in the second because otherwise you'll miss the signals that a play has changed or that a player needs you to pay attention to his/her subtle attitude cues and body language. Perhaps something you just touched on for a moment really excited them. If you're focused on getting through the presentation, you'll miss the fact that you should go into more detail on that topic.

Being in the moment is paying attention to what is actually happening, not what you've planned to happen or think will happen. It allows you to make course corrections easily and quickly when need be. That becomes crucial when there are obstacles that need your attention.

How many times have you not been fully present in the moment when talking with someone? Probably a lot. There are a couple of bad things that can result from this. First, you can miss something crucial they said or did. Whether it's a sales prospect, a boss, an employee, a friend, a spouse, or a child everyone wants to feel like they are being heard and understood and that their contributions are appreciated and their fears and objections are going be taken into consideration. However, while most people desperately want this, very few will actually interrupt you to let you know that you're not giving them what they need. They expect you to figure that out through their word choice and body language.

Think about all the times you've asked your significant other how they're doing, and they've answered "fine" or whatever the equivalent is for them. We all know from experience that one word means a whole bunch of different things. It could mean they are angry and don't want to discuss it. It could mean that they're annoyed and want you to go away. They could be feeling frightened and insecure and want you to reassure them. They could be busy or focused elsewhere and just throw it out as a placeholder or conversation ender. They could even actually be just fine. We can't just take "fine" at face value; we have to evaluate the underlying tone, the situation, the facial expressions, and body movements that accompany the word. Only then can you pick up on what they're really telling you. Even then, we get it wrong sometimes.

It can be hard enough to read the subtle cues from even the people we know well. If we have any chance of reading them off of clients, we need to be paying very close attention, not just racing ahead with the planned talk. Otherwise, you might miss the fact that your key decision-maker looked displeased when you mentioned the manufacturing timeline or that the standard color for your widget is yellow. If you had noticed, you could quickly adjust and say that there are other possibilities as far as timeline and the widget can be made in any of ten standard colors and many more custom ones. You might also pick up on the fact that they are far more interested in one of the secondary applications of your product, which you only mentioned in passing than they are the primary application. You could then go into more detail about the thing that will really grab their attention and make them want to sign with you instead of anyone else.

The other bad thing that can happen when you're not fully invested in the moment is that you can mistakenly assume you know where a conversation or a particular line of questioning is headed only to find out that you were wrong.

This can be a game breaker in business and personal relationships. I know that it can be hard. With your spouse, you've had a certain set of conversations probably dozens or even hundreds of times. With your business, there's a reason you have an FAQ. Ninety-nine percent of potential clients all have the same questions. Even if the set-up dialogue seems familiar, though, don't jump ahead. Do the other person the courtesy of hearing them out. Not only will it make them feel valued and heard, it will also protect you from some potentially crippling mistakes.

It's a dramatic example, but it illustrates the point well. A lot of couples get engaged in restaurants. A lot also break up in restaurants. For an engagement, there is often a desire for a public scene, even if it's a small one. For a breakup, there's usually a hope that the location will prevent a public scene. Both conversations start with a date and a discussion of the relationship and the other person's feelings, which often include a nervous or anxious vibe. Regardless of what you think is about to happen, this is *not* a conversation you want to jump to assumptions about because being wrong either way is devastating.

Even if your potential client seems to be asking the same question that every potential client asks, listen carefully. Just as important sometimes as the question itself can be the way they asked it or the underlying reason *why* they asked it. Knowing this can help you better answer their questions and allay their fears while making them feel valued.

So, now that you get why being in the moment is important, how do you spend more time focused on the here and now? It's not one thing; it's everything. Preparation, hours of training, and habits you form every single day, and the intentions you have can all come together to manifest this "in the moment" way of being.

Practice being in the moment while you're driving. Turn off the music or conversations that are distracting you and really pay attention to where you are and what you're doing. Practice listening to your spouse. Do more than listen; ask follow-up questions that demonstrate that you were listening and that you care about them and their concerns. You can also set an alarm for a random moment in your day. When the alarm goes off, stop and really think about what you're doing at that moment. Look at your environment in detail. What does it look, smell, and sound like? Who are you with? What's going on with them? Do they need something that you can give them right now? The more you're aware of your environment and practice focusing on what's happening at any given second, the easier it will be for you to live in the moment and get into the Zone.

"H" Zone Interview Advice

from R. Anthony - Singer/Songwriter, TV Contestant on The Voice

"They're connecting with me. [Every] time I sing and perform I make sure I smile really big, because I think there's something attractive about a smile that kind of pulls people in to you. I was smiling a lot while I was singing the song and I could tell that they were really engaged in the song. My confidence returned... But it taught me that if you really want something and believe in something, you got to have not only the skill and the perseverance to practice and make yourself better, but you got to mentally be prepared for what you're getting ready to do."

- R. Anthony

Local Tampa Bay resident R Anthony took his singing talents to season three of the hit NBC TV show The Voice. His experience and journey was absolutely incredible. He made the cuts all the way to LA to perform his blind audition on TV, in front of a 15 million viewing audience and also in front of the four celebrity judges: Christina Aguilera, Blake Shelton, Adam Levine, and CeeLo. In an amazing turn of events both Christina and CeeLo wanted him on their team.

CHAPTER 6

Zone Time Is Not Real Time

Time might stop, fly, or disappear, but it changes
completely when you're in the Zone.

We just talked about living in the moment. Now, let's take a closer look at time itself. We all know that time is a funny thing. When we were little kids a year felt like it lasted forever. When we get older, we can blink and realize that it's July and somehow it feels like it should still only be March. We can be having fun with our friends and realize that four hours have gone by in the blink of an eye. That same four hours might seem like forty when you're waiting for your workday to end or battling with insomnia in the middle of the night. So, we've all experienced time in different ways.

When you are in the Zone, something bizarre happens with time. It can pass seemingly almost in slow motion, in which each second feels like forever or it can make it feel like almost no time passes at all when in reality hours go by. I've experienced both and they are equally cool and freaky.

When playing football, there's something special that can happen when you're in the Zone. For instance, I'll be running and looking at my quarterback. It's like we're communicating with our minds. Everything around me seems to slow down and become crystal clear. I have a totally clear perception of where everything is and where I'm supposed to be, and everything slows down. It's like a slow-motion dream, where it's just a weird state. I can see the ball leave his hands and it's like it just takes its time coming toward me. I have plenty of time to adjust my position, get my hands up where they need to be. I watch the ball land in my hands and it's like I can't miss because everything is so clear, and I feel like I have more than enough time to react.

I've also had the experience where I had almost no concept of the passage of large amounts of time while I was in the Zone. I can be working on a project, meeting with clients, doing a proposal for an incentive program, or writing a script for a TV show that I'm producing and hosting, and I get so involved in that project. All of a sudden, I come out of my Zone and I look at the clock and I'm shocked to find that I've been doing this for five and a half hours, and it seems like it was only ten minutes. So, time becomes different. There is no sense of time; time doesn't become a drag.

Remember when you were in school and you'd have an hour class and a boring teacher who could make that hour seem like two days? The minute you say, "Oh my goodness, how much time left before I get out of here?" you're done. You're not going to be in the Zone. How much longer for this to be done, how much more time left? If you're focused on time, you're not focused on the right thing and you will not get into the Zone. When my oldest daughter, Alexis, started college, I warned her not to ever say, "Oh, I just want this to be over. I want this semester to end and be over."

When you do that, you become focused on trying to rush to the end, and when you get into a rush mode, you're not being here in the moment. This is where some of the elements of the Zone work together. Yes, 100%

focus is important to getting to the Zone, but it has to be 100% focus on what you're doing right now and not what you want to be doing three months from now. When you focus on rushing through to get to the end, then that is the end. You lose your productivity, and bad things can happen.

So, yes, time changes when you're in the Zone. While you are trying to get to the Zone, you still have to respect time. Be present in the moment; don't be trying to rush through it because you're bored or tired. Stop watching the clock because it pulls focus from whatever it is you're trying to do or supposed to be concentrating on.

"H" ZONE INTERVIEW ADVICE

from Nick Friedman - Founder/President of College Hunks Hauling Junk & Moving

"We were always brought up to follow the traditional career path. You get a degree, you get a job, you climb the corporate ladder. So that's what we did. About six months into it, I was just feeling really unfulfilled. I couldn't picture myself doing this for another 10, 20, 30 years of my life. So I emailed Omar and said, 'Hey, what's our timeline for starting College Hunks on a full-time basis?' And he emailed me back all capital letters, 'My timeline's right now,' exclamation point. So, we quit our jobs and started." - Nick Friedman

Nick Friedman's path to multimillion dollar success centers around junk removal. He co-founded College Hunks Hauling Junk & Moving company, and has grown that company into a dominant national franchise with over 100 franchisees across the country and gross annual revenues over 100 million. Nick has been named among the top 30 entrepreneurs in America under 30 by Inc. Magazine. He has appeared on the Oprah Winfrey Show, ABC's Shark Tank, Bravo's Millionaire Matchmaker, The Pitch, and CNBC's Blue Collar Millionaires, among many others.

CHAPTER 7

Self-Confidence and the Absence of Self Doubt

"The future depends on what you do today."
—Gandhi

In the Zone, there is no time for hesitation, second-guessing, or doubt. You just act, confident that you can do what you're attempting to do. It is a loss of self-doubt and a gain of self-confidence. It's that moment when you get out of your own way. You stop overthinking and instead trust in your skill and preparation to carry you through.

As human beings, we often listen to that inner critic, that voice of doubt inside us that talks endlessly and sabotages us. You know the one. It likes to say things like: *don't blow this. You're not good enough. You don't deserve this, you won't get this, this won't happen.* That voice is a liar. Unfortunately, we've been conditioned since childhood to listen to it. When we listen to it, we give in to fear, uncertainty, and doubt. We feel inadequate for the task before us and that feeling actually becomes a reality in our lives.

You have to have self-confidence—that absolute belief in your own abilities and your capacity to get the job at hand done. Now, that's not arrogance or lack of humility. It's not about having an attitude that says, "Look at me, I'm the greatest." Self-confidence is quieter; it's not concerned with what other people are doing or saying. You're doing your thing, playing your own game. You're not worried; you're just confident and flowing. You know you've got this and so you do.

In the business world, when you've got a product, a service that's second to none you have confidence. You know you can deliver for your client. You're doing the right thing for their best interest. And that's what it's all about.

The biggest competition you have is yourself. The biggest challenge you have is in your mind, to control what's happening in there. Whether you need to teach yourself to be more disciplined or more open-minded, or you need to learn new skills this is the opponent you need to wrestle with. Most importantly, you can't let self-doubt creep in. It becomes so very easy to sabotage ourselves and we have to fight that. When you have true self-confidence and let go of sabotaging self-doubt then you are ready for the Zone.

When you are in the Zone, all the negativity and the distractions that come with it just fade away. If you're an athlete, you don't give a crap about someone reporting what you're doing, or how you're doing it. You're not worried about the fans. You're not worried about how you look. You have no regard for the critic either external or internal. You're not judging yourself or having conversations that include things like "What if I did this wrong?" or "What if my presentation doesn't look good?" Instead you have no self-consciousness and you become detached from the end result, the outcome.

We each have around 60,000 to 70,000 thoughts a day. Unfortunately, half those thoughts are the same every day. Sometimes, they're empowering, and sometimes, they're negative. But when you have no concern about the end and judgment from the end, you're free to let it all hang out and just do your best and not have that self-sabotage of doubt enter your mind. This is one of the most critical prerequisites to you finding your Zone!

I missed playing my entire junior year of high school football because of a leg injury, torn ligaments. I couldn't walk for three months. Rehabbing and getting back on the field was an ordeal. For my first game in my senior year, there was a lot of self-imposed pressure and all these great expectations of me. I caught a few passes during the game. Then came a moment: we were on the line of scrimmage and we were at our opponents' four-yard line. My quarterback, Joey DiGirolomo (Joey D), called an audible at the line of scrimmage. He was going to throw the ball to me. I had no coverage on me, and he saw that! It should have been an easy TD.

But then I got up in my head. I realized I had a chance to score a touchdown and I said to myself, "Don't drop this ball." As the play unfolded, I kept saying that to myself. It was a nice day, perfect conditions, and there was no one around me. It should have been the easiest pass in the world to catch. When the ball came to me, I dropped it. Of course, I did! That's because I was fixated on the wrong thing. I was sabotaging myself. When you tell yourself or anybody, "don't" do something, you actually bring the image of what you don't want to happen to your mind. That moment still haunts me to this day. Even though having studied self-talk and knowing why I dropped it, the pain is still there. Lesson learned!

You can't let negative self-talk into the conversation. When you say to yourself "don't," you are opening the door of consciousness for what you don't want! Does that make sense? Here's an example. Don't think about a pink elephant.

And what are you seeing in your mind right now? The pink elephant.

When you let that negative talk in, you're allowing self-doubt to creep in and you sabotage yourself. There's no room for that kind of talk in the Zone. When Michael Jordan goes for the game-winning shot, he's not thinking to himself, "Don't miss this shot." Of course not! He's all in. He pictures what he wants instead.

So, jump forward a year to when I'm a college freshman. The team had a great year, and the opportunity arose for me to have my first college touchdown. We were on the opponents' five-yard line and my quarterback, Ron Meehan, called my play and was going to be throwing to me. I thought to myself that this was destiny and I was going to "go for it!" Only, it wasn't going to be nearly as easy a catch as the one the year before should have been.

You see, we were playing in a rainstorm with thick mud and high winds. The ball was incredibly heavy from the rain and mud. I was running in mud, struggling. People completely surrounded me. The wind was blowing the rain horizontal. The quarterback threw it, and I caught it for a touchdown. There was every obstacle against me and I can't even tell you how I caught that ball. All I know is that I told myself I was going to do it and I did. I had absolute certainty, no doubt—I was in the Zone. You see how your mind can either help you or hurt you? You decide!

Years later, when making the sale to Procter and Gamble, it was the same thing. Everything seemed to point to it being a lost cause, but I had no doubt. I had clarity of vision, went for it, and got the contract. Whether it's sports, business, the art world, or any other endeavor, you have to lose that self-consciousness to progress to a higher level.

"H" ZONE INTERVIEW ADVICE

from R. Anthony - Singer/Songwriter, TV Contestant on The Voice

"It's important to have people around you that will encourage you, too, because sometimes we put more weight on what we're saying to ourselves as opposed to people who are giving us the right feedback."

- R. Anthony

Local Tampa Bay resident R Anthony took his singing talents to season three of the hit NBC TV show The Voice. His experience and journey was absolutely incredible. He made the cuts all the way to LA to perform his blind audition on TV, in front of a 15 million viewing audience and also in front of the four celebrity judges: Christina Aguilera, Blake Shelton, Adam Levine, and CeeLo. In an amazing turn of events both Christina and CeeLo wanted him on their team.

CHAPTER 8

Defining the Outcome and Why It's Important

"Keep your face to the sunshine and you cannot see a shadow."
—Helen Keller

You can't be in the Zone if you don't know what it is you're trying to do. It's just that simple. For us to perform at our peak, we have to understand what it is we're trying to accomplish. You can play around with a football all you want, toss it in the air, run around a field carrying it, but unless your brain knows what it's trying to achieve, it can't do so at peak efficiency.

Your brain controls your entire body. It tells what muscles to activate when, what direction to move in, how deep breaths should be to get enough oxygen, how fast you need to move to get to where the ball is thrown, even whether the person next to you is on your team or an opponent you need to avoid.

We are hardwired to want to win. For our ancient ancestors, the difference between winning and losing was often the difference between life and death. We had to know what to run away from, what to run to, who

35

was on our team, and how to successfully achieve goals in order to just eat and stay alive.

Despite what it sometimes feels like, football games and even business deals are not a matter of actual life or death. However, our brains are still programmed to think in those terms. That's why we need to define things clearly for ourselves if we want to be able to get the best results from our physical and mental efforts. Our brains need to know what winning looks like so they know what the goal is and can proceed toward achieving it.

How do you know if you've won? Whether you're playing a game, climbing the corporate ladder, or trying to create your perfect life, you have to have a clear objective. In a football game, you win by having scored more than the opposing team when time runs out. In the corporate world you've won when you reach the apex of your company or your profession or whichever your target job is. In life, you win when you achieve the thing you've been striving for: a certain salary, a relationship with the person of your dreams, the house you've always wanted, etc. Sometimes, you even get something tangible to mark the victory such as a trophy, a signing bonus, or a wedding ring.

To be in the Zone, you have to have that same clarity of vision—that same understanding of what the desired outcome is. You have to know where you're going. Any time you're doing any planning, you have to start at the end, and look at the end result. You have to see what you're expecting. Then, you work back from that end result, from that vision.

When I was playing football, I knew where I had to be, what I had to do. I knew my target and the play had already been diagrammed on the chalk board and in my mind from repetitive practice and visualization. It was just a matter of the physical execution. Sometimes, during execution things have to shift to take into account unexpected obstacles, but you still need a strong understanding of where you need to end up.

It's the same in business. You need to know where you're going. Let's say that you're an entrepreneur or you're in sales. Ask yourself: what are your objectives for the year? How about the quarter, the month, the week? You take those and work backward to determine what daily activities you need to do that will ultimately get you there. I always write these goals down because by doing so you force them to be real and not moving targets that you can change when things get overwhelming or when you're worried about the challenge ahead.

If you need to, share these goals with people that can help you stick to them even when it would be easy to let it all slide. Sometimes, it can be helpful knowing that you're not just accountable to yourself but that you'll also have to explain to someone else why you chose to put off something you were supposed to do.

Once you know your goal, the most important thing is attaching your why to it. That's what keeps you going through the hours and hours of practice and work. Passion alone isn't enough. You do anything for twenty hours in a row or weeks on end and at some point that passion gets worn out. You need to be able to hold in your mind your intention, what you're doing and why you're doing it.

Whatever you're doing needs to be planned and strategized. You also need to make sure you have a balanced approach. You need to be able to have a clear objective of the whole and not just one component of your game.

Work, or business, is one component of what you're doing in your daily life. It's an expression of you because you spend a third of your life working. You need to be intentional with it. But the same goes for other areas of your life including your family, your health, and your financial wellbeing, basically all of the energy that you need to draw from.

Take your health, for example. You need to define the outcome; what is it you want to accomplish and why? Then you need to work backward. What kind of food do you need to be feeding yourself? What kind of exercise and how much of it should you be getting? How will you get yourself into a peak performance state so you can function as a businessman, an athlete, a spouse, or parent?

Every area of our lives must be clearly defined in this manner. I call it the Wheel of Life. There's your health, spiritual, family, and personal growth components. You need to get a game plan and analyze what you're doing, how you're doing it, and clarify your objectives with each. Are you taking the time to analyze the life you are living? If you could change things, would you? What would that be? Maybe consider taking some time away from watching so much TV and investing that time by watching over the life you want to live.

We can all agree that Tiger Woods was at one time the best golfer in the world. His results spoke loudly right? When he was at the top of his game, there was a point where he decided to reconstruct his golf swing so he could improve his game even more. I was stunned. Here you had one of the best golfers in the world, and he was challenging himself to deconstruct his game and then reconstruct it. Are you kidding me? That's amazing!

What can we as entrepreneurs, businesspeople, salespeople, people with a product or service to deliver learn from this? We should take away that whatever we're doing, we need to have awareness of what we're doing and how we're doing it and keep challenging ourselves and redefining our objectives. What are we going after? We need to assess and analyze every area of our business and our life. We need to look at the strategies we need to change and figure out what we need to do to make those changes. Then we can form new habits to make it happen.

It all comes back to clarity and focus and taking that quiet time to sit down and say, "What are we doing and why are we doing it?" You have to have your reasons and you have to attach why your goal is important to you. And you have to have three or four different anchors or reasons why. If your why isn't big enough, when it gets tough, you won't commit all the way through.

"H" ZONE INTERVIEW ADVICE

from "H" John Mejia - Entrepreneur, Marketing Guru, former Football Player

"I went to the top of Federal Hill Park in Baltimore's Inner Harbor. I brought a pad of paper and sat on a park bench overlooking the beautiful Harbor Skyline. For three hours I designed and mapped out my vision of what I wanted for my life. I clearly stated what I wanted to do in all areas of my life. How I wanted to feel, What value I wanted to bring to the world. I took the driver's seat back and realized I was not a victim of my circumstances. ... [That] dream list I wrote was written on the future I wanted to see, not the circumstances that [were] all around me. This is critical in having vision."

- "H" John Mejia

CHAPTER 9

It's Easy Because You've Already Put in the Time

"If it doesn't challenge you, it doesn't change you.
Personal growth always comes in the challenge."

Whenever someone achieves greatly and does the seemingly impossible, you'll hear it said that they're in the Zone. When someone catches an uncatchable ball or does a week's work in a single afternoon, it can be attributed to being in the Zone. What's more, they make it look easy because in that moment it *is* easy.

For them.

Why?

Because they've already done the hard part.

When you're in that Zone, in that peak performance state, that Nirvana, everything becomes effortless. Your movement becomes a flow. It becomes easy. For athletes, their running, their maneuvering, and other physical abilities just come easily. For businesspeople, salespeople, and entrepreneurs, they know they're in the Zone when everything is just rolling and going their way. It's like you can't fail. Whether you're giving a presentation, you're on the phone cold-calling, you're pitching investors, or hiring employees, it all feels natural and you know you're at the top of your game. It's the same for writers when they get in the groove and the words just flow through their fingers or for students who spent hours studying and just breeze through the exam.

That effortlessness of movement, persuasion, performance, and creation lets you know you're in the Zone. That's where we want to be all the time, in the moment, in the flow. We want everything that we are doing to be effortless. It's not a grind!

Of course, we can't get to that place of flow without first putting in a lot of effort and going through that grind. Now, very few people enjoy the grind. But it's something we have to do to get to the place where we want to be. You can grind yourself physically and emotionally. That grind is discipline. While it can be frustrating and even boring, we have to go through it to get to the easy part.

I wake up at 4:45 a.m. and get on a bike. I don't want to do it. I'd rather be in bed, but I force myself to be disciplined, to get up (which is the hardest part), and get started. Then, halfway through my workout, I realize that I'm doing well and I'm in the Zone. I become glad that I'm doing it and there becomes an ease of movement, a flow and rhythm that work with me to help me accomplish what I'm trying to do. I don't get there, though, without forcing myself out of bed and onto that bike.

We all have images of Michael Jordan playing at his peak. He's not forcing that ball. He's magical. He's in the Zone. We see it with all the great athletes when they're in the Zone. It's effortless. In the highest level of the Zone there is ease. You can't get to it, though, unless your mind and body have already put in the hours and years of practice and are prepared for it. Without that initial effort, there can be no ease.

One of the best examples I have of this involves Tai Chi. Have you ever seen an old person on the beach or in the park practicing Tai Chi? They've been doing it for years and there is a beautiful, simple flow to all their movements. It looks effortless, easy, like anyone could do it. I decided I would try, because if they could do it, so could I, right?

Wrong.

I hadn't put in the years of effort. I couldn't do what they did. I signed up for Tai-Chi classes and I didn't even last through three of them. It was so much harder than I could have imagined. My friend Bobby had warned me, too, that it wasn't going to be as easy as it looked. I should have listened. I was watching people who were in the Zone, who had worked to master their craft and earned their place there, and I was assuming that I could do the same thing with none of the effort.

You've heard it said that it takes 10,000 hours of effort to truly master something. While the time required can vary, the underlying idea is solid. You need to have conditioned your mind and your muscles to be able to do something without having to belabor the process mentally. Remember how many times you had to practice tying your shoe and how many times it went wrong when you were a kid? Eventually, though, your fingers get used to the motions and you don't have to pay attention to what you're doing anymore. It just happens.

When you're in the Zone, you can operate at peak performance because you've already spent the months and years needed to train your body and mind to operate on that level. Just because you finally achieve being in the Zone isn't a reason to stop either! Practice makes perfect and there are other peaks to climb. You've achieved the pinnacle of what you are capable of. But in another year of effort and practice, imagine how much more you'll be capable of? There are constantly new mountains to ascend, which is why you must always push yourself forward.

"H" ZONE INTERVIEW ADVICE

from Kevin Harrington - Creator of the Infomercial, original shark on *Shark Tank*.

"So Mark Burnett came out...he says, 'Kevin, look, forget about the 16 cameras. Forget about (the) 150 person crew. For filming know you have the best audio, the best lighting, you've got people helping the people that are pitching and they are doing all the setups...just put blinders on. You do this every day, don't you Kevin? So when they come out, just act like it's another day at the office.' And that was a brilliant piece of device from Mark Burnett. I never had any anxiousness, any nervousness. I was ready to go."

- Kevin Harrington

Kevin Harrington, an original "shark" on the hit TV show Shark Tank, is the creator of the infomercial and pioneer of the As Seen on TV brand. His work behind-the-scenes of business ventures has produced over $5 billion in global sales.

CHAPTER 10

Anticipation of the Obstacles / Adversities Are Easily Overcome

Don't be afraid to give up "good" to get to "great".

Obstacles and problems arise. That's life. Sometimes you can't predict it. You can't forecast it. Just know that every once in a while, you're going to get punched in the face and you will get knocked down. There are a lot of obstacles that are predictable, however. You might not know *when,* but you do know *what* could happen.

In an earlier chapter, we discussed being in the moment and the dangers of anticipating what another person is planning to say or do. What's different here is that we're talking about actually figuring out what could go wrong long before you show up to the game or the meeting. If you've practiced and played out worst-case scenarios on the field and in the boardroom, then you are ready for the most likely disasters and won't be caught off-guard if they transpire.

When you're in the Zone, you've already prepared for different possibilities, different outcomes. Obstacles might get thrown at you, but because you know that's a possibility, you are ready for them. You can anticipate what could happen and then overcome it easily when it does.

Of course, again, this doesn't happen without preparation on your part. First you have to be willing to acknowledge that not everything might go according to plan. Then you can make alternative plans. You're prepared, you're aware, and it makes you unshakeable.

It's like living here in Florida. I live in the Tampa Bay area. I know that the storms will come. I know the heavy winds and rainstorm conditions will come. I know it's a part of the gig of living in Florida. I know that evacuating because of hurricanes is part of that deal. Not having a plan would be preparing to fail. I know where I would go if I had to evacuate. In my garage, I have shutters to be able to go and shutter up the house. During hurricane season, I keep on hand the tools and provisions needed to shelter in place. I'm prepared. Things are going to happen. I don't know when. I just know sometimes it's going to happen. This way, because I have prepared, it won't throw me for a loop. I'll be able to do the things that are needed quickly and easily to prepare my home and family for the storm.

It's the same in business. You have to anticipate that there will be problems. Expenses will come in higher than expected. Sales will go cold. You have times when you're reaping but then there are times when things are lean and mean and you still have to keep sowing. When unpredictable things do happen, know that every great businessperson, every great salesperson, every great entrepreneur, has obstacles. The great ones are the ones that are able to navigate through those obstacles. Just know they will come. It's not going to all be smooth sailing or a cake walk into the end zone. You're going to have obstacles all along the way getting there.

You're not always going to be in that elite performance-range of the zone. Just know you're going to have days when you don't feel like it, when it's going to be a struggle, you have no flow, and everything is sluggish. It's the grind and things are happening. That's just life.

I always seem calm, but, believe me, there have been times when I wasn't. I've had times when things seem to be going well until they took an unexpected downturn and I didn't react properly. I was unprepared for disaster from a business point of view and a human one as well. Everyone makes mistakes. It's important to own up to them, face them, and then move on because they are just speedbumps on the way to the Zone.

When you're in the Zone, adversities that come before you are overcome with ease. They are no big deal. They are little minor bumps in the road. You make your adjustments in that flow. The minute something goes bad, you have two paths. You can either have self-doubt and reinforce it, or you can continue to maintain your crystal clarity of your vision, your objective.

I remember another one of the great sporting experiences I had. We were down twenty-eight to nothing. It was fourth quarter with eight minutes left in the game. Sounds dismal, right? But something magical happened to our offense. We started getting angry and upset at what was going on. We became fed up at our poor play. Then it started; we just took it one play at a time. We went down the field, and suddenly it was 28 to 7. We had our vision. We can do this. We talked about the comeback. We went down the field again and it was 28 to 14 then 28 to 21. Finally, it was 28 to 28. We tied the game. In 8-minutes we did more than we could do in 3 and 1/2 quarters. You never know when the Zone can show up for you. You only need to keep trying regardless of the circumstances.

When the adversities mount up, there are so many examples of great players, great quarterbacks stepping up. Think about Tom Brady. He shows us great examples, right? He doesn't give up. No matter what's happening, whether he's down or he's up he maintains that crystal vision all the way to the end.

When you're in the Zone, obstacles are just bumps on the road. You don't take a little bump. And you know, sometimes in our minds we magnify that obstacle and we create our own self-doubt. We make that obstacle become Mount Everest and we self-sabotage. If you keep the vision, at least you know where you're going. So, use it as inspiration, motivation, anger, the football demon, whatever, just drive forward.

"H" ZONE INTERVIEW ADVICE
from Kato Kaelin - Actor, Radio and Television Personality, Businessman

"Pain makes you grow, and as you know anybody that's gone through grief, it's a process you have to deal with the grief. You can only get stronger. I've lost both my parents... Grief is just part of life. You've got to have grief to grow." - Kato Kaelin

Kato Kaelin gained international fame as a witness in the O.J. Simpson murder trial. Kaelin is an actor and television personality. He started his own company selling loungewear.

CHAPTER 11

Balance of Skill Set and Challenge

Every day is a new beginning.
Take a deep breath, smile, and start again.

When you're in the Zone, you are being challenged and it will push you to the edges of your abilities. To reach the Zone, there has to be a balance between your abilities and the difficulty of the task you're facing. In relation to your skill set, the challenge can't be too easy but neither can it be impossible.

For example, if you have a college football team playing against a bunch of twelve-year-old Pop Warner kids, then there really is no challenge. The college football team is going to score like twenty-touchdowns, but the players will never get in the Zone because they're not being pushed to be their best. If you're not challenged, you'll never get to that peak performance place of challenging your talent for expansion for the Zone.

Conversely, if you're the Pop Warner team, the challenge is too great. It's not realistic that even if everyone played at the top of their game that the team could possibly win. The challenge is too great to be overcome by the skills of the players so they will never reach the Zone.

The same principle holds true in the business world. Say you're an entrepreneur starting out and you haven't yet made even $30,000 in your own business. If you want to try to step into the arena and go sell a Fortune 100 company a billion dollar deal, it's just not going to happen. For the skill set you possess, the challenge is just too great. It's not realistic. I'm not saying to not go for it, but you have to have a challenge that's realistic in order to expand yourself.

I remember our football team used to be the underdog going to play universities that were bigger, stronger, and faster. Everything on the books would show them that we didn't have a prayer. But that's the challenge, right? We're the same age and we all put on a helmet the same way. Even though the other guys would be bigger and faster we'd decide it was a challenge that we could take because the gap wasn't too far. And you know what? We won more than any of those teams would have guessed. We had enough skill and the challenge was just great enough that it could help push us into the Zone and we would rise to the challenge.

You have to have a long shot and the potential to grow and maximize your skills in the moment. That's when you can get to the Zone. If it's too hard or too easy you'll never get there. It's all about the balance. In fact, it's critical to have a balance of expectations.

"H" ZONE INTERVIEW ADVICE

from Phil Albert - former Head Football Coach, Towson University

"As an achiever once you win, you want to do it again. We set our sights on let's continue to get better, let's continue to work hard. The whole thing with me was to speak into the life of those players that we had. Relate to the players and I am going to invest my life into them. Individually we probably were not very talented but together we believed. We were a lot better together than we were individually."
- Phil Albert

Phil Albert is the winningest football coach in Towson University history. He was named Kodak District II Coach of the Year three times.

CHAPTER 12

The Real Reward Is the Struggle, Not the Prize

Life is only a reflection of what we allow ourselves to see.

The final element or aspect of the Zone is that when you're in that place, don't focus on the prize. Focus instead on the struggle that you are engaged with in that moment. Sounds crazy, right? Well, remember, the Zone is all about blocking out distractions and being completely in the moment. Thinking about what you're hoping to achieve out of all this won't help you do either when you're actually in the Zone.

Let's say you're an entrepreneur and you want to win entrepreneur of the year. You want to be in *Time* magazine. You want to be on the *Entrepreneur* magazine cover with your trophy in your Lamborghini. That's fine, but that can't be your focus. I mean, the focus of what you do needs to be driven by a pure passion for what you're doing, for sharing your message, sharing your products, sharing your service to the world. That's where the reward is. It's in that journey. It's in that struggle of raising money or working on a shoestring budget, presenting your strategies, working through competition, challenges, building your customer base, and building your employees if you decide to go that route. Being in the Zone is not about focusing on the end goal; it's about loving what you're doing every single day and rising to the challenges and going through the adversities.

I remember, as an entrepreneur in the early days, we had built our company to a $15 million dollar company. I remember the days that we had to go through struggles, go through layoffs and cutbacks. I remember my partners and I would have to run to the bank and plead with the banker to cover payroll. We had a quarter million dollars of expenses every week. *A quarter of a million!* We had times when we didn't take paychecks for months. We wanted to make sure the employees got paychecks. There were times where we wrote personal checks to cover it ourselves. Had we been in it focused on some sort of reward, we would never have made it through. Instead, we were focused on meeting the challenges as they came.

The reality is the reward is in that struggle. It's in the doing. The reward is in that process and who you become during the journey. Acknowledgement is great, but it's just a fleeting moment. It's who you become during that process that can never be taken away. When you break through and reach a certain level, a certain skillset, have a certain group of experiences, that can never be taken away from you. You become that new person that reaches a new level, and it enables you to embark on the next journey, to push for the next peak performance, strive higher and better and have more and different and vaster experiences.

It's not about getting to the finish line because it's an ongoing journey. There is no actual finish line, right? There are new horizons, new levels, new strengths, new challenges, new wounds that we have to have healed to strengthen us, to position us to where we're going as part of the game.

So, it isn't about winning the Super Bowl, being Entrepreneur of the Year, or making a million in sales. Those things are great, but the reward is the byproduct of the journey, the self-sacrifice, the battle you've fought. The reward is not the focal point. If everything is based on your happiness, to get the plaque and be recognized or getting a multi-million dollar home, then you're going to miss it. The fulfillment will not be there. That's because you're going to say, "Wait a minute, I thought I wanted this. Is this really all there is?" Exactly.

I have a client who had a goal of getting a Lamborghini. He fixated on it, and worked for it, and wanted it so badly. Then, once he got it, he was asking that same question: "Is this really all there is?" He discovered, like I did, that fulfillment comes not from the reward but from the journey. When you're in the Zone, the reward is not your focus. It's all about the here and now; that's the music that's being created in the flow.

"H" ZONE INTERVIEW ADVICE
from Marcus Allen - Football Analyst, Former Professional Running Back

"No one would understand this, but it's the guys, my teammates. The bus rides. The working hard together. The fun, the laughter! The special moments we all shared together. That's what I value most! No one will really understand that."

- Marcus Allen

Marcus Allen is a former football running back for the Los Angeles Raiders and the Kansas City Chiefs. and a football analyst for CBS.

CHAPTER 13

It's Transitory

"[The top of the mountain], I got a taste of it and it's literally a fleeting moment. It leaves you, so I'm stuck with this disappointment. What do I do now to top that? ... Then it comes to me. My time is going to come."
—R. Anthony

Once you've gotten a taste of the Zone, you're going to want to stay there all the time. The unfortunate truth is you can't. It only lasts a short while. Those who have prepared for it, though, get to spend time there more frequently than everyone else. That might seem crazy unfair. I mean, if you're at the top of your game, why can't you stay in the Zone?

The short answer is because nothing ever stays the same. Change is always happening. Downturns are inevitable, but you have to learn to work with those as well to minimize them and to get right back to the peak. There are factors that are going to be beyond your control: injuries, relationship issues, market crashes. Plus, let's face it: no one can give 100% every second of every day indefinitely. Eventually, you will burn out and if you're not prepared to handle the downtime, it can kill you.

The Summit

Let me give you an example. Over the years, I've had an interest in Mount Everest. I'm always fascinated to hear about climbers who challenge themselves to go to Mount Everest, to go through that, and to climb the summit. These climbers go to 27,000 plus feet above sea level and go to the death zone where the air is super thin and it'll kill you up there. Your body spends more oxygen than it can take in and you only have minutes before it will collapse.

It's not just the lack of oxygen that's a problem, either. There are dangerous, treacherous paths riddled with challenges. You can fall. You can freeze to death. You can be injured and trapped. You can get buried in an avalanche. You can have a heart attack. There are many different ways to die on that mountain and hundreds have. Yet, people still make the climb. Why?

To get to the top.

As far as pinnacles go few can argue that this is one of the greatest both physically and psychologically. For anyone who has ever wanted to push themselves, test their limits, this is the ultimate challenge for mind, body, and spirit. Climbing it is a testament to one's will and courage. And apparently the view is pretty great, too.

Getting to the top takes a lot of preparation and conditioning. You spend six weeks getting your body adjusted and ready before you can even begin to approach the summit. Then you have to spend the same time coming down. If you stayed at the summit for more than a small window of time, the oxygen deprivation alone would kill you in a matter of hours.

There's a sign at the bottom of the mountain that says *respect the mountain*. You have to respect the Zone. It's a beautiful place to be, but it's very easy to get hurt. You do not own that mountain. That mountain can turn on you with weather conditions and if you're sloppy, unprepared, or unlucky, you can die.

It's the same in the Zone. You don't own the Zone. You can only own the moments that you create in the Zone. Those moments do not last forever. Just like reaching the summit, you reach that pinnacle experience, that high for a moment. The majority of your time is preparing for climbing and then descending from the Zone.

All great athletes can tell you this. No one spends all of their time in the Zone, no matter who they are. Michael Jordan always says that he blew the game winning shot 26 times. He lost almost 300 games in his career. But all his failures are directly related to his great career because he kept taking the shot. He knew that even when he wasn't at that peak state, the highest level, he had to keep going through those levels of downturn.

The Business Summit

When you get to that peak performance state that is known as the Zone, Nirvana, whatever you want to call it, things are flowing in business. Companies are growing. You're hiring employees; you're generating sales. You might go from $100,000 to $200,000 to half a million dollars. Now you're a multimillion-dollar company producing 5 million, 10 million, or 15 million in sales. I've been there. I've been through that journey. I've been on that road.

The reality is, that highest level of performance, when you're riding it, ride it, maximize it, stay in the Zone. Sales are happening, the market's good. Conditions are good. Double down on it because there's always a wave. It's like the stock market. We know there's going to be ups and downs like undulating greens on the golf course. It's just part of the game. So, we have to realize that when things are riding high, we need to take advantage of it, and prepare for those unexpected times that come down.

In business, as we strive to reach our Mount Everest of opportunity, to reach our Mount Everest of performance, we need to be prepared for the fact that it's quite the journey to get there. Many companies might die along the way, particularly if they haven't prepared. Athletes have to train for three months before they even head out to Everest and they have to condition themselves. When they get there, it takes them about a week or two just to travel to the Mount Everest base camp. When they're at their base camp, they have to go up and down the mountain for six weeks and acclimatize their blood cell count as they're going up to the higher altitudes and then coming back down. They do that for six weeks before they even attempt to approach the summit. And then, finally, after weeks of preparation, of those who are remaining, who have not gotten sick or blood clots or whatever's going on, those who attempt to get to the summit, only a small fraction make it. Once they are there, they're on top of the world. They have that view above everything. Highest point in the world, and they're standing looking down at the clouds, right? All the way, they have to stay fixated on the goal.

As a business owner, you want to make your first hundred thousand dollars of income or your first million dollars of income. You want to stand on that zenith that you've defined as your Mount Everest. You know during that journey how many people start but never make it. They're getting fired, they're burning out, their business is collapsing, and they're not able to progress.

Those that do make it achieve their goal and get that mountain top moment, which is like nothing else. You're on top of the world. But you've only got a short time to enjoy it. Getting there is only part of the journey. There are more peaks to climb, but first you have to get your butt back down the mountain because most of the treachery, the deaths, and the bad things happen on the way down, because people get exhausted. It becomes about maneuvering your way back down safely. Then, you regroup.

When you're out of the Zone, it's time to ready yourself for your next big goal, your next venture whether it's in life or sports or business. For a while at CMC Meridian, I set my mind on getting the Salesman of the Year Award. That was the zenith, the summit that I was chasing.

I remember the first one that I won. It was a great year; bonuses, productivity, the awards' party, a big plaque, and recognition at the awards' dinner were all awesome. Both my mom and dad were there to witness it, and I was able to honor them at that awards ceremony. I decided to take that award and have a chance to shed light on my parents. It was just so awesome and perfect.

At the end of the wonderful evening, I had one sales rep say to me, "Watch your back. I'm coming after you. I'm going after that award next year."

I was blown away. I'm like, "Wait a minute. You have to be kidding me. I'm at the top. I'm at the summit. I won. Can't you give me some time to enjoy this?"

You know what lesson I learned in that moment? It's the journey and the process of doing it that's the greatest gift of all. And you know what? That moment is quick; I had it and it's done, right? That Zone of perfection does not last forever. It might last for a game. It might last for a presentation. It might last for a week, a month, a year. There's a short time to it. Just acknowledge it and know that the peaks and the highs are all part of the experience. And your greatest lesson is that the journey and the process are just as valuable, more valuable even. Whether I was standing on stage with my trophy or holding the football aloft in the end zone after a touchdown, amazing as it was, it was just a moment.

When you're in that peak performance state, whether you're a salesperson, an entrepreneur, or an athlete, that highest level does not last forever. That peak performance is a peak, right? And behind a peak on the other side are different levels. You have to leave one peak to reach the next one.

"H" ZONE INTERVIEW ADVICE

from R. Anthony - Singer/Songwriter, TV Contestant on The Voice

"[The top of the mountain], I got a taste of it and it's literally a fleeting moment. It leaves you, so I'm stuck with this disappointment. What do I do now to top that? ... Then it comes to me. My time is going to come. These are moments of preparation for me. These are moments of development for me and when that climax, when my season comes where I'm out there and I'm doing this for life, I'm on the big stage and I am sharing my music with the world, it's going to be at the right time."

- R. Anthony

Local Tampa Bay resident R Anthony took his singing talents to season three of the hit NBC TV show The Voice. His experience and journey was absolutely incredible. He made the cuts all the way to LA to perform his blind audition on TV, in front of a 15 million viewing audience and also in front of the four celebrity judges: Christina Aguilera, Blake Shelton, Adam Levine, and CeeLo. In an amazing turn of events both Christina and CeeLo wanted him on their team.

CHOOSING TO *STEP* ONTO THE FIELD

"In the end, it's not the years in your life that count. It's the life in your years."
—*Abraham Lincoln*

When choosing to do anything new, the first step is the most important. It's the one that changes your world and literally reshapes reality around you. You can't get into the Zone if you never even get into the game. To get into the game, you first have to step onto the field, whatever that field it is. Whether it's a relationship, a business, a sport, or financial health you can only perform well if you choose to step up and try. Take action!

Growing up in my neighborhood, sport was a big deal. Not just football, but anything kids could get together. And play we did! I wasn't naturally talented. I wasn't the biggest or fastest by any imagination. I could have looked at the kids in my neighborhood, who had the physicality and the talent, and decided that I couldn't, wouldn't play. Sometimes, people don't want to play because they don't think they can win or because they're afraid of losing or looking foolish or being made fun of. Some people only try things they're sure they'll be good at. That's a mistake.

You see, when I started out, I wasn't good at football. In fact, I was often picked last when it came to teams. I didn't let that stop me, though. Every day, I chose to step onto the field. I chose to play the game. That first day, that first step forward led me all the way to signing an NFL free-agent contract years later. Imagine if I had never taken that first step?

I've applied that same principle to everything else I've done. I wanted to start a business. I wanted to get into sales. I wanted to work in television. I wanted to write a book. Every single time I had no experience, no reason to think I would succeed. Every single time I took that first step and that has made all the difference in my life. Whatever it is you want to do, whatever you want to achieve, you must first decide to step up.

CHAPTER 14

How Do You Get There?
Step into the Zone!

It's not about what you wish for, but rather what you go out and work for.

Everyone has dreams. Some are realistic, others aren't. Everyone's dreams have one thing in common. They won't come true without work. Wishing and hoping needs to be backed up with planning and doing. Yes, I know—that sounds a lot like work. But if your dream isn't worth working for, then it's not much of a dream.

The way you get from where you are to where you want to go is baby stepping. You don't have to make gigantic strides. All you have to do is take the first small step. Then, once you've done that, take the next. Then, the next after that, and so on.

You don't have to start with a grand business plan. You don't have to spend months figuring it all out. You don't have to spend money renting office space or equipment or hiring people. All you have to do is choose to take the first step forward, no matter how small it is.

Nick Friedman, the President and co-founder of College Hunks Hauling Junk and Moving Company, remembers the humble first step that he and his partner took. They were off college for the summer. A family member loaned them a beat up van and ordered them to use it in some way to make money instead of loafing around on their summer break. After much discussion, they realized that they could charge people to haul their junk away. They took the first step in this bold business venture: they came up with the name. Then, they took the second step: they printed fliers and put them in people's mailboxes.

A lady wanted to hire them. She had a backyard full of stuff that needed to be cleaned out. They showed up at her place (step number three). They had no idea what to actually say when she wanted to know how much they'd charge. So, they picked a number: $200 (step number four). She agreed and they set about to start grabbing stuff (step number five). Almost immediately, it began pouring rain and they had a choice before them. Did they give up at this first obstacle or did they push forward? They decided to keep going and clear out her junk like they'd just agreed to do. That was step six. Just like that, they were in business. Within a few years, they had built their company into a national brand with over one-hundred franchises across the country. How did they do that? One step at a time.

Every successful entrepreneur has a similar story. One moment, they weren't in business; all they had was a dream, an idea, a thought. Then they took a positive step to put things in motion, to make that idea a reality.

One small step is all it takes to get started. Here's the catch, though. You are the one who has to make that step. You have to choose to do something. Even if you're lucky enough to have someone offer you a dream opportunity or ask you to partner with them, you still have to say "yes" and make a positive step forward to accept the opportunity and begin working at it.

Whenever starting something new, whether it's a new sport, a new business, a new career, you can't expect to knock it out of the park on your first day. Those steps that you take all build upon one another as you learn and grow in your new endeavor. First, you step onto the field. Then you start playing the game in earnest. You progressively get better and better at it, expanding your knowledge and skills. Then you reach that level of peak performance. You step into the Zone where you are functioning at your highest level. However, you'll never get there without that very first step.

"H" ZONE INTERVIEW ADVICE
from Darren Prince - Sports Agent, Writer, Speaker

> "A lot of it is smoke and mirrors when you're in that startup mode because you have to trim the expenses, you have to have the image that you are successful... Surround yourself with people that are more successful, that can teach you from their experiences, that you can learn from and save you years of financial hardships. And that's what I started doing. I just surrounded myself with people that I looked at as mentors in the industry and I just became a sponge." - Darren Prince

Darren Prince is a legendary sports and entertainment agent who started his career as a kid when he built a multi-million dollar business selling baseball cards.

CHAPTER 15

Get on the Field

There's never going to be a perfect moment, a perfect time. The solar system's not going to align with perfection for you to take action.

The hardest step in any journey is the first one. If you want to play the game, though, you have to show up to the first day of practice. You can't just sit at home wishing you were on the team. If you want to go into business, you need to make a first affirmative step. You can't step into the Zone until you step up.

Choose to Move

Whatever you accept and tolerate in your life will continue on. Nothing ever changes unless you take action. No amount of wishing and hoping is going to change your life without you taking an affirmative step, putting yourself out there.

Most people never leave their comfort zones unless thrown out of them kicking and screaming. The truth is we are creatures of habit. We only change if we are motivated by deep desire or unbearable pain.

If we never move, though, we miss out on so much. There are so many life experiences and opportunities that come when you just commit to taking a step, even if it's a small one.

Growing up in Queens, New York, I was very fortunate at the age of nine to move into a neighborhood where the guys that were around me were older, bigger, and stronger, and they loved sports. So, I had no choice but to be involved in sports playing everything from Wiffle ball to baseball to touch football. Sports gave me the ability to learn discipline, to have tenacity to continue to do and try and practice and practice because, as I mentioned earlier, I was not naturally gifted. My neighborhood friends will tell you. I was terrible. I was the last guy that would get picked if I even got a chance to play. Yet, there was something that was attractive to me about sports—the work ethic, the discipline. I just kept trying and practicing and practicing. I kept challenging myself.

Over the years, I focused more on football. It ultimately provided me many great opportunities from Pop Warner, to high school football, a scholarship toward college football, the opportunity to sign an NFL free agent contract with the Indianapolis Colts to have an opportunity to go to mini-camp and training camp with an NFL team, the experience to sign with two USFL football teams as well. I've met some incredible friends through those experiences, and it was very, very enlightening. I treasure those sports experiences that I had at every level.

None of that would have been possible if I hadn't committed to trying. I got on the field, starting when I was a kid. Even though I was the youngest, smallest, weakest, and least gifted in my neighborhood, I tried and look how far I got. You don't have to have started things when you were a kid, though. It's not too late to commit to doing something regardless of your age. Grandma Moses didn't start painting until her seventies. What if she had decided she was too old to do something new and never tried? My TV career didn't start until I was in my thirties. The hardest thing you'll ever do is choose to take that first step, so don't sabotage yourself by choosing to take it and then delaying. Take that step right away.

No Perfect Time to Start

People always like to pick start dates that they think are meaningful. They'll start a diet on Monday because they want to enjoy their weekend. They'll start new habits on January 1st because the fresh, shiny New Year seems like a good time to become a new them or turn over a new leaf. Plus, who wants the hassle of changing and being uncomfortable over the holidays? Or they pick triggering events. They'll do something after college or when the kids are out of the house or after they retire. The problem is that one day you wake up and a decade or two or four has gone by and you're still no closer to doing whatever it was you wanted to do in the first place.

The truth is that picking a date in the future to start anything is too late. That's right, because *today* is the day to start. How many times do we say, "I'll do it tomorrow, I'll get to it tomorrow?" The reality is we said that yesterday, so today is the day to do some things and take action.

There will never be a perfect time. There will never be a perfect time that you're going to have all the money you need to start a business. There will never be a perfect time to have all the conditions aligned for you to start marketing your product, or your services, or whatever business you want to get into. You need to remove the phrase "I'll do it when …" from your vocabulary. That's because "when" doesn't exist, it's just what people say when they can't be honest enough with themselves to say "never."

So, there is no "when." There is only today. You have to start now. Start small. You can take action, even if it's minor. This is probably one of the most powerful things I can share. Even if you start by allocating ten minutes a day, so you just sit down and take the focus, time, and attention to start planning, start thinking, start getting excited about what you want to do, what type of business you're in, want to get in, or if you're an existing business, if you just took ten minutes a day, you can start moving toward that dream of building your own business or taking an existing one to the next level.

They say that the best time to plant a tree was twenty years ago and the second best time is now. That's so true. If you have an aspiration that you want to take control, you want to expand your income circle, you want to start a business, or you want to become an entrepreneur, then start now, start today. The years that you put in and the hard work will manifest your tree and opportunities will be there. But you have to start by planning and getting things to happen.

Choose to move. Start immediately. That's how you get into the game and that's how you choose to STEP into the Zone.

"H" ZONE INTERVIEW ADVICE

from Julie Weintraub - Founder of Julie Weintraub's Hands Across the Bay Charity

"As small business owners, we have always made contributions back to the Tampa Bay community. There was a defining moment years ago, where we made a contribution towards a particular charity and later learned that a good portion of their fund raising budget went to cover operating expenses and only a small % of the dollars donated actually (went) to help those in need. Steve and I were shocked and so frustrated that we were donating to organizations but really didn't know how the money was spent. That inspired us to go start our own foundation where we could provide complete transparency and get those dollars to those in need. That was over 10 years ago, and today we continue to grow our charity efforts and help those who need a helping hand up." - Julie Weintraub

Julie Weintraub and her husband, Steve, own the Gold and Diamond Source jewelry store. Julie's charity helps domestic violence survivors and those who have been blindsided by emotional and financial turmoil and need a hand.

CHAPTER 16

A Small Play is Better than No Play

"Don't be pushed around by the fears in your mind.
Be led by the dreams in your heart."
—*Roy Bennett*

Start Small

When preparing to do anything new there are a few things that people get hung up on. One of them is deciding *when* to do something (which we've learned is TODAY) and the other is figuring out *what* to do. The first step trips up the vast majority of people, keeping them from ever stepping foot on the field. The second step scares away or injures many of those who do take that step forward.

Everyone thinks that you have to start big, that you have to do something dramatic or nothing at all. That's simply not the case. Ten minutes a day is enough to start with on anything. If you can spend more time, great, but don't fool yourself into believing that small effort is the same as no effort. The path to the Zone is not a sprint, it's a marathon. You can't just jump in, do a flurry of things, and expect to achieve total success right away.

When starting a business, I usually advise people not to quit their day jobs at first. Don't go out and hire employees and lease office space before you bring in a single dollar. It's better to start at a desk in your home, even if it's in your garage, and focus on the essentials first. Start small and then build from there.

I built my TV video production agency from scratch while I was running other companies full time. If I can do it, so can you. In the evening, you have opportunities to get away from the TV set and take time. You have hours at nighttime to do some work, and you can commit to building your dream. You can figure out what you need to do, what you want to do, how you want to monetize it, what product, what service you want to provide. Just watch less TV and start building your dream.

A Simple Idea is Good Enough

Oftentimes, the best ideas are the simplest ones. Yet, somehow, we always have trouble believing that. We come up with an idea and we think, "That's too simple, that's not good enough." We worry that it isn't fancy or isn't high tech.

Honestly, a simple idea that has a vision and is well executed will work ten times better than any fancy, elaborate idea you never get around to executing. Simple ideas have the added advantage of being easy to explain to customers, employees, strategic partners, and investors.

Come up with your simple idea and then come up with a simple plan. Then, take action to start developing it. What's your company name and logo? Once you figure that out you can create a Facebook page and a simple one-page website in just a couple of hours. You can use an online printing company like Vistaprint to get a stack of business cards for twenty bucks.

Once you commit, things come together that allow you to start taking the idea, the concept, and manifest it into reality, and start making it happen. You start small, and then you can start building as you go along.

You can start marketing as you go along. Find that one product, that one service, that one idea that you can market, bring to the marketplace, and monetize. Do it and start getting paid for it.

You don't have to wait until you have twenty-five products to offer out there. Neither do you have to wait until you know everything. Just get started.

Back in college, one of my coaches owned a roofing company. It was a family business. During the summer, I used to go to a neighborhood, knock on doors and hang door hangers promoting the roofing business. I would drive to a neighborhood, get out of my car, hustle, walk down the neighborhood, meet people, shake hands, and promote the roofing business. We'd get roofing jobs and I used to get a fat commission check. I knew nothing about roofing, nothing about the products or the process. All I did was market the services, and when the deal went through, I'd get a nice 15% commission check.

I didn't need all the education or all the experience in the world. What I needed was the willingness to hustle, to go out on those hot summer days and talk to people. That's what it's all about. It's getting out there in the marketplace and making people aware of what you're doing.

"H" ZONE INTERVIEW ADVICE

from Nick Friedman - Founder/President of College Hunks Hauling Junk & Moving

"Business is a journey. No 'overnight success' is going to happen overnight. Back then I wanted the world yesterday, and so I would tell myself to just have patience. You know, life is a long time. The combination of time and effort is eventually going to produce results… So don't try to shortcut success, because there are no shortcuts."

- Nick Friedman

Nick Friedman's path to multimillion dollar success centers around junk removal. He co-founded College Hunks Hauling Junk & Moving company, and has grown that company into a dominant national franchise with over 100 franchisees across the country and gross annual revenues over 100 million. Nick has been named among the top 30 entrepreneurs in America under 30 by Inc. Magazine. He has appeared on the Oprah Winfrey Show, ABC's Shark Tank, Bravo's Millionaire Matchmaker, The Pitch, and CNBC's Blue Collar Millionaires, among many others.

CHAPTER 17

Don't Be Afraid to Throw a Hail Mary

"Strength and growth only come through continuous effort and struggle."
—Napoleon Hill

Some people get caught up in trying to have a perfect plan and executing it. Even the best, most well thought-through plans can fall apart. On the flip side, sometimes the craziest, most ill-advised plans can result in success. The point is, you can't let a lack of knowledge, skill, or field position bench you. Sometimes, you just have to act.

Do Something Crazy

Crazy action can be better than no action at all. That's because the universe rewards boldness. Most people never put themselves in the game. Just by doing something, anything, in furtherance of your dreams, you've already separated yourself from the vast majority of people with a similar dream.

One of my companies is a TV video production agency. I purely got into that space years earlier when I saw an ad in the newspaper looking to hire an on-air reporter on a cable TV channel in Cincinnati, Ohio. They wanted to have a reporter out there in the community to deliver stories.

Well, guess what? That wasn't my major in college, and I was already working in sales. I was in my thirties, and I had zero experience in mass communications let alone being an on-air TV personality. I saw that ad, though, and thought that it would be really cool to do that. So, with zero experience, no demo reel, no portfolio, I went to the casting call. I was actually completely clueless about what it normally took to get that kind of job. Sometimes not knowing too much is good!

I went to the casting call and I was in line with other people who all had work experience in TV. They had their resumes and demo tapes with them. All I had was my ambition and energy. I walked in, talked to three show producers that were doing the interviews. In three or four minutes, I left. When I walked out, I said, "Well, that didn't go very well." All I left with them was a VHS tape (back in those days) with a video I made where I just spoke to a hand-held video camera. By all rights, when you saw who I was up against, I should have had no chance.

They called me a few days later, and actually gave me the opportunity. It turned out that even though I had zero experience, they really liked my energy. I got the job because I didn't know enough not to go. Thank goodness! I went, which was a complete Hail Mary move. Sometimes, you have to go for it, no matter what. You might not have the experience. You might lack qualifications. You might look around and see that you're outclassed by the competition in every way. All you can do in that moment is push yourself out of your comfort zone and dare to be you. Let your personality shine and give it everything you have. Take the shot!

On paper, it was a crazy move. There was no way I should have even tried for that job. I did. I got it. It changed my life. You have to constantly assess where you are. What do you want to do? I thought this was something that looked interesting and decided to pursue it. As a result of me doing something that was crazy, it opened up the door for all the TV shows I've done and produced, and the celebrity interviews I've done, the people I have met, the locations I have seen. All that just because I took action and took the shot.

Move Forward Regardless of How Much You Know

No matter what area of your life or what your career or business ambitions, you will spend a lifetime learning. In fact, most successful entrepreneurs are lifelong learners, absorbing as much information on a wide variety of subjects as they can. You've got a lifetime ahead of you to hone your existing skills and learn new ones. There will always be someone who knows more than you. Just when you think you know enough, then you'll discover that you've just scratched the tip of the iceberg. That is a fact, not an excuse.

Never let a lack of knowledge stop you from moving forward. There's never going to be a perfect moment, a perfect time. The solar system's not going to align with perfection for you to take action. You've just got to go out and do it and make some things happen. So many people are afraid of making mistakes, so they never take that leap. Guess what? You're going to make mistakes no matter how well-prepared and knowledgeable you are. In fact, it's one of the best learning tools there is.

Step forward with enthusiasm, optimism, and a willingness to learn as you go. That's more than half the battle right there. Continue pushing that envelope of what you know and what you can do every day in pursuit of your dreams. Have confidence that what you need to know you'll figure out along the way. Don't wait, take that first step now!

"H" ZONE INTERVIEW ADVICE

from R. Anthony - Singer/Songwriter, TV Contestant on The Voice

> **"You got to believe. You have to believe in yourself. That was really big for me, because there's so much pressure and so much conversation you have with yourself. You could really talk yourself out of an opportunity."**
>
> **- R. Anthony**

Local Tampa Bay resident R Anthony took his singing talents to season three of the hit NBC TV show The Voice. His experience and journey was absolutely incredible. He made the cuts all the way to LA to perform his blind audition on TV, in front of a 15 million viewing audience and also in front of the four celebrity judges: Christina Aguilera, Blake Shelton, Adam Levine, and CeeLo. In an amazing turn of events both Christina and CeeLo wanted him on their team.

POWER TIP #1
TAKE RESPONSIBILITY

*"Self-pity is our worst enemy and if we yield to it, we
can never do anything wise in this world."*
—*Helen Keller*

Here's something to keep in mind as you work your way forward. No one is responsible for you but you. No one has the responsibility to make you successful or to get you in the Zone. No one has the responsibility to drag you there and to make you into a top performer. You need to be responsible for all that yourself. You need to be accountable to yourself.

You are where you are right now based on decisions and actions or lack of actions that you did or didn't take to get you to this point, right? All those cumulative decisions, thoughts, and actions have brought us exactly to where we are in this specific moment in our life. So, the success we're experiencing in all areas of our life, not just the sales game or business, is because of the decisions we've made.

So, the reality is: things happen. We all have stuff that happens to us and sometimes life can beat you up. Life can condition you to get into a blame game. Could have, should have, would have—we all have excuses. But the reality is when you own your success, you own your performance, own your results, own what you're doing, then you have power. You don't give away your power.

Maybe you got a bad rap or a bad deal. Okay, so what? Those are all part of the game. You need to take responsibility for yourself in order to get into the Zone, to be at the highest level for your business, for your sales, for your entrepreneurship, and your spirit. You need to be accountable and take responsibility. Once you are able to accept it, that you do have the power to make changes, then you get on a different path heading to that breakthrough result.

This is really important because high performance people do have thoughts of doubt and fear, and they do sometimes dwell on things or worry about things. However, what makes them a high achiever is that they're able to move through all of it and deal with it. The thing is: when you shift blame, you're losing power. That's right; you're surrendering your power and becoming a victim, powerless.

About fifteen years ago, I was traveling a lot, crisscrossing the country. I was sitting in traffic and I was exhausted from traveling. Things were not working out so well; some scenarios were not ideal. I started fixating on all that and started feeling sorry for myself. I looked out the side of the car and I saw a blind gentleman who was walking with his seeing eye dog and a cane. We're in L.A. with traffic and it's just him and his dog. Talk about a reality check! Here I was healthy, had the ability to go out and drive around. We should always be grateful because there are those who don't have what we do and would love to be as blessed as we are.

Helen Keller was someone who was deaf and blind, and she blows me away with all she accomplished. She would say that, "Self-pity is our worst enemy and if we yield to it, we can never do anything wise in this world." This is coming from a woman who couldn't see and couldn't hear. How's that for a little perspective! We should all take responsibility for our lives. We have the ability to change our mindset. We have power to change our course and change our direction.

Who's responsible?

You are.

Who's responsible for your success?

You are.

Who's responsible for your failure?

You are.

Who's responsible for how much effort you put into things?

You are.

Who's responsible for your attitude no matter the circumstances?

You are.

Who's responsible for turning bad into good and good into great?

YOU ARE!

POWER TIP #2
THINGS CHANGE WHEN YOU CHANGE

There are a lot of clichés about change. We've all heard that the only constant in life is change. Chances are you've also heard that the more things change the more they stay the same. A lot of pessimists will even gleefully tell you that people don't change. The truth is that change, of some sort, is inevitable. The universe is constantly moving toward entropy. That means that without outside effort, things tend to decay and fall apart.

If you want proof of this, look at your life. What happens if you don't take care of your body? It decays and falls apart. What happens if you ignore your relationships? You wake up one day and the people in your life are strangers or, worse, not even there anymore. The same is true in every area of our lives including business.

In order to combat this, we all put in effort. Oftentimes, whether we want to admit it or not, it's the minimum amount of effort to maintain, to keep things going. Put another way, we put in just enough effort to keep ourselves stuck in patterns that have been playing out in our lives for months, years, and even decades. Take a look at your body, your key relationships, your work, and your mental and spiritual health. Take a good, long look. If you don't do anything different from what you're doing right now, ten years from now, these will all look pretty much the same. They might even look a little worse for wear as age takes its toll.

Does that scare you? It should. Ten years from now, do you want to be where you are now financially, physically, spiritually? If the answer to that is "yes" then you clearly have no interest in pushing yourself to be your best. (Which begs the question, why are you even reading this book?)

If the answer is "no," then you need to figure out what you need to do to make ten years from now, ten months from now, ten *minutes* from now different from now. How do you bring about change? How do you push yourself toward your peak performance, toward the life that you want?

Delatorro McNeal told me the story about a guy walking down a road. In the distance, he hears a dog howling in pain. As he gets closer, he sees a house. The dog is still howling while a man sits on the porch, not doing anything.

The traveler asks what is going on. The man on the porch says the dog is sitting on a nail. The traveler asks him why he isn't helping the dog and removing the nail from it. The man's reply says everything. He says that when the dog decides it hurts badly enough, he'll stand up by himself and get off the nail.

We've all been that dog. We've all been injured in our health, our business, our finances, our relationships. That's just part of life. We all have stuff that happens to us. The question is, how long do we stay in that pain? How long do we stay in that adversity and howl about it but don't actually move? At what point do we decide to rise up, move off the nail, start shaking it off, and start going in a different direction? Nothing is going to change for that dog until he decides to make a change and get up.

Things change when you change. They change when you commit to changing what you are doing. When you want something different, don't expect something outside of you to change. Change comes from within and radiates out. You need to change your mindset, your motivation. Then you change your habits and your activities. Then everything around you changes in response to the new stimuli.

So, don't expect reading a book or having a conversation with a boss or a spouse to change your life. You need to assess yourself to see what needs to change inside you. Then, when you are ready to change, you have to make the decision to do so. Only then do you empower yourself and push yourself toward that peak performance. Only then do you change your life.

One defining moment, one decision, and one action changed the course of my life. I went to an open casting call for an on-camera TV field reporter position. I had no experience and no training. I was already in my 30s. Many times during my life I have self-sabotaged myself with limiting beliefs. Fear and doubt have often times left me paralyzed and prevented me from taking action. There have been moments I have lacked self-confidence to proceed on things. Thankfully, this time, I didn't think too much. I just went to the casting call and took a shot.

Guess what, they liked my personality and gave me a shot on TV and were willing to work with me. Even though I had no idea what I was doing! That small step of faith opened the door for me to a career in television and media. As a result of that, during my career I have worked with some of the biggest corporate brands and many well-known celebrities and professional athletes.

What about you? Have you ever talked yourself out of doing something because you felt you weren't good enough? Not smart enough? Not talented enough? That's happened to me so many times! Look at the journey and what I would've missed had I stopped myself from going to that interview.

If I can do it, you can, too! Step into your Zone! Go for the things you want to do and be!

Here are a few pictures of the incredible people I have interviewed and the memorable experiences I have had because I had the courage to take that first small step.

Kim Kardashian with **'H' John Mejia** in LA on Fox Sports at Celebrity Golf Party

Actor **Alfonso Ribiero** with **'H' John Mejia** in LA on Fox Sports at Celebrity Golf Event

NFL Hall-of-Famer **Terrell Owens** Interviewed by **'H' John Mejia** on Fox Sports

Actor **Jeremy Piven** from HBO Entourage with **'H' John Mejia** and **Deanna Brooks** on Fox Sports Celebrity Golf Party

Actors **Ashton Kutcher** & **Demi Moore** interviewed by **'H' John Mejia** at Super Bowl Charity Event

Actor **Kevin Connolly** from HBO Entourage with **'H' John Mejia** and **Monica Leigh** on Fox Sports

TV Star **Kendra Wilkerson** with **'H' John Mejia** in LA for Celebrity Golf Event on Fox Sports

NFL Hall-of-Famer **Deion Sanders** with **'H' John Mejia** at Super Bowl Good Life Tampa Bay TV Show

NFL Hall-of-Famer **Marcus Allen** Interviewed by **'H' John Mejia** on Fox Sports

TV Host **Nancy O'Dell** with **'H' John Mejia** at Vegas Television Convention (NATPE)

Boxing Champ **Evander Holyfield** with **'H' John Mejia** at Celebrity Super Bowl Golf Event

Actor Comedian **Kato Kaelin** Interview with **'H' John Mejia**

Actors **Esai Morales** and **'H' John Mejia** at LA Celebrity Golf Event

Fox Sports TV Special with **'H' John Mejia** at Playboy Mansion Celebrity Golf Event with **Ajay Pathak**, President of Playboy Golf

NFL Hall-of-Famer **Warren Moon** and **'H' John Mejia** on Fox Sports

TV Host **Robin Leach** and **'H' John Mejia** at NATPE Convention in Vegas

Actor **John O'Hurley** from Seinfeld with **'H' John Mejia** and **Tom Carmody** on Fox Sports TV Celebrity Golf

NFL Hall-of-Famer **Derrick Brooks** with **'H' John Mejia** on 'Good Life Tampa Bay' Covering Tina Jackson Fashion Event at BUCS Stadium

TV Host/Comedian **Bill Maher** with **'H' John Mejia** on Fox Sports LA Celebrity Golf Party

Baywatch Actress **Traci Bingham** and **'H' John Mejia** at LA Celebrity Golf Fox Sports

ESPN's **Dick Vitale** and **'H' John Mejia** on 'Good Life Tampa Bay' for Tampa Charity Event

NFL Hall-of-Famer **Lawrence Taylor** and **'H' John Mejia** at Super Bowl Golf Event

Ali Boxing Trainer **Angelo Dundee** with **'H' John Mejia** for Interview for Movie Producer Penny Marshall

MLB Player **Joe Carter** and **'H' John Mejia** at Super Bowl Celebrity Golf Event

Actress **Brande Roderick** and
'H' John Mejia at Fox Sports LA
Celebrity Golf Party

NFL Player **Mike Alstott** with **'H'
John Mejia** on 'Good Life Tampa
Bay' for Charity Event

Actor/Singer NSYNC **Joey Fatone**
and **'H' John Mejia** at Fox Sports LA
Celebrity Golf Party

NFL Player **Anthony Fasano** and
'H' John Mejia on Fox Sports LA
Celebrity Golf Event

Actress/Entrepreneur, HSN-QVC Personality **Rhonda Shear** and **'H' John Mejia** 'Good Life Tampa Bay' TV Interview

NFL Player **Roger Craig** and **'H' John Mejia** at Super Bowl Pre-Game Party 'Good Life Tampa Bay' TV Show

Boxing Champ **Vinny Pazienza** and **'H' John Mejia** on Fox Sports LA Celebrity Golf Party

NFL Player **Kellen Winslow** and **'H' John Mejia** on Fox Sports LA Celebrity Golf Event

NFL Player **Shelton Quarles** and **'H' John Mejia** on 'Good Life Tampa Bay' TV Show

NFL Player **William Floyd** and **'H' John Mejia** on 'Good Life Tampa Bay' for Charity Event

NFL Player **Richie Incognito** and **'H' John Mejia** on Fox Sports LA Celebrity Golf Event

NBA Player **Matt Geiger** and **'H' John Mejia** on 'Good Life Tampa Bay' for Charity Event

Playboy Playmate/Radio Host **Pilar Lastra** and **'H' John Mejia** on Fox Sports LA Celebrity Golf Event

Playboy Playmate **Stephanie Glasson** and **'H' John Mejia** Fox Sports LA Celebrity Golf Event

Tampa Mayor **Pam Iorio** and **'H' John Mejia** on 'Good Life Tampa Bay'

Radio Personality **Orlando Davis** and **'H' John Mejia** on 'Good Life Tampa Bay' TV Special of 'Tampa Bay's Dancing with the Stars'

NFL Player **Tony Parrish** and
'H' John Mejia on Fox Sports
Celebrity Golf

NFL Players **Kenyatta Walker** and
Ryan Sims with **'H' John Mejia** on
Fox Sports

NFL Player **Miles Austin** and
'H' John Mejia on Fox Sports LA
Golf Event

NFL Player **Mike Sherrard** and **'H'
John Mejia** on Fox Sports

ABC Action News Anchor **Jamison Uhler** and **'H' John Mejia** on 'Good Life Tampa Bay' TV Special 'Tampa Bay's Dancing with the Stars'

NFL Player **Michael Clayton** and **'H' John Mejia** on 'Good Life Tampa Bay'

NFL Players **Jason Bell** and **Marcellus Rivers** with **'H' John Mejia** at Fox Sports LA Golf Party

TV Dance Judge **Mary Murphy** and **'H' John Mejia** on 'Good Life Tampa Bay'

NFL Player **Jim Weatherly** and **'H' John Mejia** on Fox Sports

Actress Hollywood Legend **Elke Summers** and **'H' John Mejia** on Fox Sports Celebrity Golf

Actor **Glenn Plummer** with **'H' John Mejia** on Fox Sports Celebrity Golf Event in LA

Actress **Deanna Brooks** and Heather Kozar with **'H' John Mejia** on Fox Sports Celebrity Golf

Fox 13 **Charley Belcher** and **'H'**
John Mejia on the 'Good Life Tampa
Bay' TV Show

NFL Bucs Owner **Bryan Glazer**
and **'H' John Mejia** on 'Good Life
Tampa Bay'

Actor/Comedian **Tommy Davidson**
and **'H' John Mejia** on Fox Sports
LA Celebrity Golf

MLB Player **Darrel Evans** and
'H' John Mejia on Fox Sports
Celebrity Golf

Playboy Mansion in LA with **'H' John Mejia** on Fox Sports

NFL Player **Sterling Sharpe** and **'H' John Mejia** Super Bowl TV Special Golf Event

Steve and Julie Weintraub with **'H' John Mejia** on 'Good Life Tampa Bay' TV Show

Radio Personality **Pete O'Shea** and **'H' John Mejia** Interview

Publisher **Bridgette Bello** and **'H'** **John Mejia** on 'Good Life Tampa Bay'

Fashion TV Personality **Tina Jackson** and **'H' John Mejia** on 'Good Life Tampa Bay'

Entrepreneur **Nick Friedman** with **'H' John Mejia** on the 'Business Zone' TV Show

Actor Comedian **Larry Joe Campbell** with **'H' John Mejia** on Fox Sports LA Golf Event

Tampa Entrepreneur **Aakash Patel**
with **'H' John Mejia** on
'Good Life Tampa Bay'

Actor **Roger Cross** with **'H' John
Mejia** and **John Pulitano** on Fox
Sports Celebrity Golf Event

NFL Player **Takeo Spike** with **'H'
John Mejia** on Fox Sports

News Anchor HSN TV Personality
Rebekah Wood Co Hosting
'Good Life Tampa Bay' TV Show with
'H' John Mejia

Original Shark **Keven Harrington** from ABC Shark Tank TV Show with **'H' John Mejia** on the 'Business Zone' TV Show

NFL Player **Willie Gault** with **'H' John Mejia** on Fox Sports Celebrity Golf Event

National TV Fox Sports 'Skyball' W with TV Host **Brian Dunkleman** with Celebrity Judges **'H' John Mejia** and Radio Personality **Meredith Andrade**

Actor **Daniel Baldwin** with **'H' John Mejia** on Fox Sports LA Celebrity Golf Party

MLB Player **Jose Canseco** and Actress **Brande Roderick** with **'H' John Mejia** on Fox Sports LA Celebrity Golf Event

Actor **Kevin Dillon** from HBO Entourage with **'H' John Mejia** Fox Sports Golf

General Norman Schwarzkopf with **'H' John Mejia** on 'Good Life Tampa Bay' TV Show

E! TV Stars **Holly Madison** and **Bridget Marquardt** with **'H' John Mejia** on Fox Sports Celebrity Golf

Radio Interview with **Spiro Morekas** and **'H' John Mejia** at USF-Towson Game

NFL QB **Jeff Garcia** with **'H' John Mejia** on 'Good Life Tampa Bay' TV Show

Entrepreneur **Usman Ezad** and **Dr. Dinar Sajan** with **'H' John Mejia** on 'Good Life Tampa Bay'

'H' John Mejia and Production Team for Fox Sports TV Show on LA Celebrity Golf

Towson Tigers at the USF Game-
**Gordy Combs, Bill Logan, Spiro
Morekas, 'H' John Mejia**

NFL QB **Jay Cutler** with **'H' John
Mejia** on Fox Sports Celebrity Golf

MLB Player **Jim Layritz** with **'H'
John Mejia** on Fox Sports Celebrity
Event

NFL Player **Simeon Rice** and **'H'
John Mejia** Interview

NFL Player RB **Reggie Bush** and **'H' John Mejia** Interview at Moves Magazine Party

NFL Player **Randy Cross** and **'H' John Mejia** Pre-Game Party Interview

NFL Player **Phillippi Sparks** with **'H' John Mejia** Interview at Super Bowl Party

Singer **Sandra Denton** (Salt-N-Pepa) with **'H' John Mejia** Red Carpet Interview

On Set Fox Sports Skyball TV Special
with **Brian Dunkleman**, **'H' John
Mejia** and **Meredith Andrade**

TV Reality Stars **Gretchen Rossi** and
Slade Smiley with **'H' John Mejia**
Fox Sports Interview at Celebrity
Golf Event Party

Bruce Jenner and **'H' John Mejia**
Interview at Celebrity Golf Event in LA

Kim Kardashian and **'H' John Mejia**
on 'Good Life Tampa Bay' Super
Bowl Special

Wild on E! TV Host **Art Mann** and **'H' John Mejia** on Fox Sports Celebrity Golf Party in LA

NFL Player RB **Ricky Waters** and **'H' John Mejia** Super Bowl Party Interview

P Diddy Combs with **'H' John Mejia** Red Carpet Interview on 'Good Life Tampa Bay'

NFL Player and ESPN TV Host **Marcellus Wiley** with **'H' John Mejia** on Red Carpet Interview

Boxer Winky Wright with 'H' John Mejia Interview

TV Actor Clifton Davis and 'H' John Mejia Red Carpet Interview

Tampa Bay Bucs Cheerleaders at QB Jeff Garcia Charity Event with **'H' John Mejia** 'Good Life Tampa Bay' Coverage

TV Personality **Kris Jenner** and **'H' John Mejia** on 'Good Life Tampa Bay' Super Bowl Party Coverage

NFL Hall-of-Famer **Jerry Rice** with **'H' John Mejia** on 'Good Life Tampa Bay' Super Bowl Party Coverage

NFL Player **Dwight Freeney** and **'H' John Mejia** Interview

NFL QB **Jesse Palmer** and **'H' John Mejia** at Pre-Super Bowl Party Coverage

NFL Player **Brad Culpepper** with **'H' John Mejia** at Jeff Garcia Charity Event

Singer Jordin Sparks with 'H' John Mejia at Super Bowl Party Coverage

MLB Pitcher Matt Garza with 'H' John Mejia 'Good Life Tampa Bay' Super Bowl Special

Fox Sports Skyball with **Brian Dunkleman** and Celebrity Judges **Meredith Andrade** and **'H' John Mejia**

NFL QB **Matt Stafford** with **'H' John Mejia** on 'Good Life Tampa Bay' Super Bowl Special

WWE Wrestler **'Zeus'** with **'H' John Mejia** on 'Good Life Tampa Bay' Super Bowl Special

Kourtney Kardashian Red Carpet Interview with **'H' John Mejia** on 'Good Life Tampa Bay' Super Bowl Special

UFC Fighter **Tito Ortiz** with **'H' John Mejia** on Fox Sports Celebrity Golf

Kim Kardashian Interview with **'H' John Mejia** on Fox Sports in LA Celebrity Golf

Actors Ashton Kutcher and Demi
Moore with 'H' John Mejia on 'Good
Life Tampa Bay' Super Bowl Special

Model/Actress Melanie Tillbrook
with 'H' John Mejia 'Good Life Tampa
Bay' Super Bowl Special

White House Attorney and Former
Florida Attorney General **Pam
Bondi** and **'H' John Mejia** Interview
for 'Good Life Tampa Bay'

'H' John Mejia on Set at Castle
Production Studios in Burbank
California

WDAE Radio Personality **Ronnie 'Night Train' Lane** with **'H' John Mejia** on 'Good Life Tampa Bay'

ABC Action News Anchor **Lauren St. Germain** and **'H' John Mejia** on 'Good Life Tampa Bay'

Lightning Hockey CEO **Steve Griggs** with **'H' John Mejia** on 'Good Life Tampa Bay'

'Great Day Live' TV Host **Kendall Kirkham** and **'H' John Mejia** on 'Good Life Tampa Bay'

WWE Manager **Jimmy Hart** and **'H'**
John Mejia

Fox 13 News Anchor **John Wilson**
and **'H' John Mejia** on 'Good Life
Tampa Bay'

NHL Player **Ryan Callahan** and **'H'**
John Mejia on 'Good Life Tampa Bay'

Clearwater Mayor **George Cretekos**
and **'H' John Mejia** on 'Good Life
Tampa Bay'

Sports Writer **Frank Deford** and **'H'**
John Mejia

Lightning Hockey Player **Daniel**
Girardi with **'H' John Mejia** on
'Good Life Tampa Bay'

WWE/Governor **Jesse Ventura** with
'H' John Mejia at NATPE Convention

WWE Superstar **Titus O'Neil** with **'H'**
John Mejia on 'Good Life Tampa Bay'

Actress/Singer **Tia Carrere** with **'H' John Mejia** on Fox Sports Celebrity Golf Party in LA

Cincinnatti on the Go Production Studio with **Rick Boyer** and **'H' John Mejia**

NFL Player and Actor **Ed Marinaro** and **'H' John Mejia** on Fox Sports Celebrity Golf Event

Speaker and Author **Barbara Glanz** and **'H' John Mejia** on 'Good Life Tampa Bay'

TV Host **Jerry Springer** and **'H'**
John Mejia at NATPE Convention

Outback Steakhouse Co-Founder
Chris Sullivan and **'H' John Mejia**
on 'Good Life Tampa Bay'

NBA Owner and ABC TV Shark from
Shark Tank **Mark Cuban** and **'H'**
John Mejia at NATPE Convention

Singer/Actor **Lance Bass** and **'H'**
John Mejia on Fox Sports Celebrity
Golf Party

NY Yankee **Mel Stottlemyre** and **'H'**
John Mejia at Charity Event

Co-Host **Stephanie Glasson** and
Heather Kozar with **'H' John Mejia**
at Playboy Golf Miami Event

NFL Player **Christian Okoye** with **'H'**
John Mejia on Fox Sports Celebrity
Golf Event in LA

NFL Players **Christian Okoye** and
Eric Dickerson with **'H' John Mejia**
on Fox Sports Celebrity Golf Event

Fox Sports **Deanna Brooks** and **'H'
John Mejia**

NBA Player **Ike Austin** and **'H' John
Mejia** on Playboy Celebrity Golf
Miami Show

Fox Sport TV Anchor **Van Earl
Wrigh**t with 'H' John Mejia at
Celebrity Golf Event

Celebrity Agent **Darren Prince**
with **'H' John Mejia** Interview on
'Business Zone' TV Show

Radio TV Host **Jack Harris** and **'H'
John Mejia** Interview on 'Good Life
Tampa Bay'

Fox Sports Celebrity Golf with **'H'
John Mejia** and **Lisa Dergan**

NFL Player/Analyst **Booger
McFarland** and **'H' John Mejia** on
'Good Life Tampa Bay'

TV Host **Pat O'Brien** and **'H' John
Mejia** at NATPE TV Conference

Palms Casino Owner, Sacramento Kings Owner **George Maloof** and **'H'** **John Mejia** on Fox Sports TV Special

Florida Governor **Jeb Bush** with **'H' John Mejia** on 'Good Life Tampa Bay'

TV Producer **Mark Burnett** and **'H'** **John Mejia** at NATPE Convention

Fox Sports **Lisa Dergan** and **'H' John Mejia** Celebrity Golf Event in LA

NFL Player and TV Host **Michael Strahan** with **'H' John Mejia** Red Carpet Interview

Actor Dancer **Cris Judd** and **'H' John Mejia** on Fox Sports Celebrity Golf

Season 1 TV Show 'The Apprentice' **Troy McClain** with **'H' John Mejia** at NATPE

Tiger Football Movie Premiere with Former Tigers **Rodney Smith, Gerry Sandusky, Sean Landeta,** and **'H' John Mejia**

NFL Player **Nick Mangold** and **'H' John Mejia** Super Bowl Party Interview

NY Yankee Player **John Ellis** and **'H' John Mejia** at CT Charity Event

3 Penny Film Founder **Jess Atkinson, 'H' John Mejia, Sean Landeta, Joe Schreiber** at Towson Football Movie Premiere

TV News Anchor **Veronica Citron** with **'H' John Mejia** on 'Good Life Tampa Bay'

NFL Player **Ryan Nece** and **'H' John Mejia** Red Carpet TV Interview

ABC TV Host **Natalie Taylor** with **'H' John Mejia** on 'Good Life Tampa Bay'

NY Yankee Pitcher **Ron Guidry** and **'H' John Mejia** Interview at Lou Piniella Celebrity Golf Classic

ABC Action News Anchor **Wendy Ryan** and **'H' John Mejia** on 'Good Life Tampa Bay' TV Special on TBDWTS Event

TV personality **Erica Cobb** with **'H'
John Mejia** on 'Living the Good Life
Chicago' on Comcast TV

NFL Player **D'Qwell Jackson** and **'H'
John Mejia** Interview

HCSO Sheriff **Lisa McVey Noland**
with **'H' John Mejia** Interview

Former NY Yankee/Met **Darryl
Strawberry** and **'H' John Mejia**
Interview at Lou Piniella Celebrity
Golf Classic

Actor **Steven Bauer** with **'H' John Mejia** on Fox Sports Celebrity Golf TV Special

Actor **Christopher McDonald** with **'H' John Mejia** on Fox Sports Celebrity Golf TV Special

MLB Player and NY Yankee Announcer **Ken Singleton** and **'H' John Mejia** Interview

NFL Player **Johnathan Ogden** with **'H' John Mejia** Red Carpet Interview

Actor **Jim Turner** with **'H' John Mejia** Interview for Fox Sports Celebrity Golf

Former NY Yankee Player/Manager **Lou Piniella** and **'H' John Mejia**

NFL Player **Terrell Suggs** with **'H' John Mejia** on Fox Sports Celebrity Golf Event in LA

NFL Hall of fame Player **Eric Dickerson** with **'H' John Mejia** Interview

'H' John Mejia, Talent Agent **Mead Chasky** and WWE MGR. **Jimmy Hart** at Lou Piniella Celebrity Golf Classic

NFL Hall of Fame and Super Bowl Champion **Derrick Brooks** and **'H' John Mejia** at Client Conference Meeting in Tampa, Florida

Boxing Champ **Antonio Tarver** and **'H' John Mejia** at Lou Piniella Celebrity Golf Classic

Fox Sports Playboy Celebrity Golf Event in Vegas with **Van Earl Wright** and **'H' John Mejia**

TV News Anchor **Reginald Roundtree** and **'H' John Mejia** on 'Good Life Tampa Bay'

Tampa Mayor **Jane Castor** and **'H' John Mejia** at PBS WEDU Be More Awards 'Good Life Tampa Bay' Interview

TV News Anchor **Sarina Fazan** with **'H' John Mejia** Interview on 'Good Life Tampa Bay'

Kendall Kirkham TV Host of 'Great Day Live' with **'H' John Mejia** on 'Good Life Tampa Bay'

TV Personality **Erica Cobb** with **'H' John Mejia** on 'Living the Good Life Chicago' on Comcast TV

Hockey Star **Vinny Lecavalier** Interview with **'H' John Mejia** at Fashion Funds the Cure Charity Event

Chicago B96 Radio Personalities **Jobo, Erica Cobb,** and **Eddie** with **'H' John Mejia** TV Interview 'Good Life Chicago'

Miss Florida **Megan Clementi** and **'H' John Mejia** on Client TV Commercial Production Shoot

Kim Kardashian with 'H' John Mejia on Fox Sports Playboy Golf Celebrity TV Special

TV Host 'H' John Mejia at Chicago Whitesox Stadium on 'Living the Good Life Chicago' on Comcast TV

NBC News Anchor Gayle Guyardo, Infomercial King Kevin Harrington and Executive Producer Wendy Latorre with 'H' John Mejia Interview

Funny Interview with John Pulitano and Ajay Pathak from PBOY Golf on Fox Sports with 'H' John Mejia

Tampa Mayor **Bob Buckhorn** TV Interview on 'Good Life Tampa Bay' with **'H' John Mejia, Aakash Patel, Shilen Patel, Nancy Vaughn**

Fox Sports Co-Hosts **Deanna Brooks** and **'H' John Mejia** on Playboy Celebrity Golf TV Special

TV Host **'H' John Mejia** at the Fashion Funds the Cure Charity Event with BayNews 9 Anchor **Jen Holloway**

Charter Communications Team **Joe Varello** at NY Mets Games Invited **'H' John Mejia** as Guest in Their Suite

Actor **Richard Kind** Interview with **'H' John Mejia** at Playboy Celebrity Golf Event in LA

GDS and Hands Across the Bay Founder **Julie Weintraub** Interview with **'H' John Mejia** at WWE Titus O'Neil Community Event

MLB Manager, Coach, Player **Don Zimmer** with **'H' John Mejia** at Joe Torre Charity Event

New England Patriot's Center **Dan Koppen** Interview with **'H' John Mejia** Fox Sports LA Celebrity Golf Event

Business Partners **Tom Coffeen,
Brian Bell, 'H' John Mejia, Nick
Delcorso** Featured in TBBJ

UFC Fighter **Tito Ortiz** Interview
with **'H' John Mejia** on Fox Sports
Celebrity Golf Event TV Special

TV Host **Art Mann** Interview with
'H' John Mejia on Fox Sports
Playboy Golf TV Special

NBA Philadelphia 76ers Team Owner
Pat Croce and TV
Host **'H' John Mejia** at NATPE
Television Convention

Fred Williamson (Ex NFL Player, Movie Star, Producer) with **'H' John Mejia** TV Interview Celebrity Golf Event in LA

Keynote Speech for 3,000 People Booked for **Delatorro McNeal** (Speaker and Author) with **'H' John Mejia** in Chicago

Singer **R Anthony** made it to the Hit TV Show on NBC The Voice with **'H' John Mejia** - Interview on 'Good Life Tampa Bay' TV Show

Fox Sports LA Celebrity Golf Co-Hosts **Deana Brooks** and **'H' John Mejia**

Winning Team at 'Good Life Tampa Bay' Team - **'H' John Mejia** and **Brian Sawin**

Detroit Tigers Game Following a Million Dollar Account Presentation - **Tom Coffeen, Dan Cross** and **'H' John Mejia**

Former Tiger Football Teammates - **'H' John Mejia, Rich Walker,** and **Jim Peterson**

Bayside HS Football Team, Always One of NYC Top Football Programs

Towson University Tiger Football Event with Coach **Phil Albert, Coach Paul Buckmaster,** and Teammate **#14 Mike Lewns**

Tiger Football Lambert Cup Championship Co-Captains **Don Washington, 'H' John Mejia, Pat Murphy,** and **Gary Rubeling**

Team from Towson University Tiger Football Lambert Cup Champions

50 Years of Towson University Tiger Football

With My Brilliant Step-Son Alex

On the Beach in Treasure Island with
My Wife and Youngest Daughter

With my Awesome Oldest
Daughter Alexis

Mejia Family from Jamaica Queens,
New York

Some of the Dreams I Had as a Kid
Did Turn Into Reality !

From Football to Business
I Have Always Tried to
'Step Into the Zone'

MOVING *INTO* THE FUTURE

Whatever you accept and tolerate in your life will continue on.

Once you've stepped onto the field and committed to doing something to further your dreams, it's time to really buckle down into the work ahead of you. You're getting into the thick of things now. Things are coming at you, both opportunities and obstacles. Some people will be cheering you on while others will be predicting your failure. Now is the time to take a deep breath and move forward boldly. You've taken the first step. Now keep moving because there's no turning back if you want to achieve what you've dreamed of.

CHAPTER 18

Stay on the Field

Through the seed of adversity is a seed of equal or greater success.

By taking the first step onto the field, you've already accomplished more than most people. The trick now is not to throw away that momentum. You need to keep marching forward and really commit to the game. Obstacles and challenges might present themselves early on. Don't view these as game killers. View these as opportunities to up your own game and bring all your skills to play.

There is No Going Around

Everyone is always looking for shortcuts. In reality, there are very few. Almost everything worthwhile is achieved through hard, persistent, dedicated effort. This often means pushing forward when others would quit the field entirely. It also means staying the course sometimes for years before getting to where you want to go. You have to find it within yourself to keep going even when you want to stop.

Imagine you're one of the defensive guys in a football game. You job is to put pressure on and sack the other team's quarterback. You know what you want. You know how to accomplish it. Before you ever reach the quarterback, though, you've got to get through the guys in front of you whose job it is to defend that quarterback. Now, these guys on the front line are big, strong, tough, and hit really hard. They're not going to just lie down and roll over. No, they're going to make you work for every inch of ground. You probably don't have time to try and get completely around them. The only true path is through them.

When you get into the game you have to be prepared to drive forward in pursuit of your goals, even if you have to fight for every inch you gain. That takes a level of commitment that goes beyond just showing up to play. It means putting forth 100% effort every time you push forward. It means leaving everything you have on the field. It also means confronting your own fears, obstacles, and shortcomings.

Confront Your Challenges and Fears

When bad things happen, there's a very real desire to curl up and lick your wounds. When you're striving to live your best life, to perform at your top level, you can't afford that luxury. Pain and setbacks are going to come. You need to confront them head on and recognize that they also provide you with opportunities you might not have otherwise had.

Like everyone, I've had my share of obstacles and challenges thrown my way. These aren't things I seek out, but I've learned how to adapt and rise to the occasion when they present themselves. This is something you learn to do through experience.

Several years ago, my partners and I basically invested in a company and started doing video highlight shows for big corporations. We had a gentleman on the payroll in that first year who had experience with these types of things and was being more of the producer or front man who dealt with the corporations. It was because of him that we had a relationship with Playboy Celebrity Golf Tournaments. When the check finally came in from one of the big companies we did a highlight video for, this guy diverted the check and ran off with it.

Obviously, my partners and I were shocked, disappointed, and more than a little depressed. We could have let it sink the whole operation. I still had access to a network of editors and a great camera team. I reminded myself that I had on-camera experience years earlier.

I approached Playboy Celebrity Golf Tournament and I told them, "Hey, listen, we want to work with you. We're not working with that guy anymore. And guess what? The next video production in LA, we're going to do it for you for free. We're not going to charge you anything."

What that did was give me the opportunity, the window, the stepping-stone to get a video and TV career started again out of a bad situation. And that journey...that belief, that risk, is what being an entrepreneur is all about.

You go forward and you figure it out as you go along. What started out as a disaster, with someone stealing from our company, ultimately led me to a national TV show that I produced and hosted on Fox Sports. I did an eight-year run with the Playboy Celebrity Golf Tournament, and it opened up the doors for me to interview movie stars, celebrities, and athletes while producing other types of TV shows.

I have a long resume of things that haven't gone well for me. I've had struggles and challenges, like we all do. But the reality is that through the seed of adversity is a seed of equal or greater success. You might not see it, but there's always a flip side to adversity. When it hits, survival instincts kick in. The pain that you endure gets you ready for more growth and opportunities because it makes you stronger. It's the same as when you work out and build muscle. You're tearing down your muscle, you're exhausting yourself, but once you tear it down, it's in the repair of that muscle that it gets stronger.

When you go through the wringer as an entrepreneur, you come out stronger. The process helps you become a stronger person and you need to welcome it and embrace that experience in the entrepreneurial game. It's priceless. It's also unavoidable. You better have your game on and get ready because adversity is going to come at you. Just make sure to use it as a stepping stone when it does.

"H" ZONE INTERVIEW ADVICE
from Nick Friedman - Founder/President of College Hunks Hauling Junk & Moving

"If you're not persistent or willing to persevere over the challenges or roadblocks that get laid in front of you, you're going to stumble or you're going to give up."
- Nick Friedman

Nick Friedman's path to multimillion dollar success centers around junk removal. He co-founded College Hunks Hauling Junk & Moving company, and has grown that company into a dominant national franchise with over 100 franchisees across the country and gross annual revenues over 100 million. Nick has been named among the top 30 entrepreneurs in America under 30 by Inc. Magazine. He has appeared on the Oprah Winfrey Show, ABC's Shark Tank, Bravo's Millionaire Matchmaker, The Pitch, and CNBC's Blue Collar Millionaires, among many others.

CHAPTER 19

Overcoming Your Toughest Opponent, You

You do not find a happy life. You need to go out and create it every day.

The biggest obstacle you'll ever face, the harshest critic you'll ever have to deal with is yourself. That sounds crazy, I know, but think about it. How many times have you sabotaged your chances at something? How many times a week or even a day do you criticize yourself? How often do you find yourself distracted and unable to focus? Sometimes, the biggest victory you have in a day is over yourself.

Self-Sabotage

Believe it or not, there are people out there who'd like to see you fail. They're jealous of you or what you're doing threatens their comfort zone in some way or they see you as competition or a threat in some other way. There are also a ton of naysayers who would never admit that they want you to fail, but who tell you constantly that they expect you to. They remind you of all the reasons why what you want to do is hard and why you might not be up for the challenge. It can be hard to hear these things, particularly if those naysayers are close friends or family members. In all that potential sea of negativity, though, there is one person who can and will sabotage your efforts. That's you.

I know, it seems crazy, but you are your own worst enemy. You criticize yourself probably more than anyone else can. You doubt yourself constantly. You question each of your decisions, sometimes endlessly. You are so afraid of failing that you fixate on it until you practically guarantee that it's the only possible outcome. Unfortunately, that's just part of human nature. We've all had bad experiences that leave our faith shaken, our confidence shattered, and we don't want to repeat those mistakes and failures again. So, instead of focusing on all the positive things we can be doing we focus on the potential disasters and our own shortcomings.

I've had challenges. I've had bumps in the road, and I've had that cycle of ups and downs like we all do. I've experienced everything from business failures to deals gone south to bad investments. I've been on the brink of bankruptcy personally, financially, and had setbacks in my relationships in all areas of my life. During those journeys I got a chance to learn who I am. I learned so much about happiness, fulfillment, and the meaning of life. I also learned about what it takes to have confidence, which can be the greatest struggle of all.

When we face adversity, oftentimes we end up struggling with self-doubt. Our self-confidence takes a hit and all our fears and insecurities raise their ugly heads. We begin to second guess ourselves and we get into a negative feedback loop that ultimately sabotages us.

We have over 60,000 thoughts every single day. Over 50% of those are repetitive and having to do with day-to-day life. No matter how you look at it there's still a lot of thoughts you're having about yourself, your place in this world, and the goals you're trying to achieve. When we let our own fear and insecurities manipulate us, those negative thoughts can ruin our lives.

It's important to step back and gain some perspective. For ten minutes a day or a full day from time to time or longer if that's what it takes it's important to step back from the daily reactionary game and reflect on what is actually going on in your life. Where have you thrown on the brakes when you shouldn't? Or when have you raced through when you should have been slowing down to notice what was happening around you?

Time to reflect, see the truth of different situations, and choose how you will adapt and react is essential to breaking us out of our everyday, negative ways of thinking. This is the time to ask yourself the tough questions. It's also time to weed out the lies you've been telling yourself and focus on the truth of your situation instead. Stop, take a time out, and get everything under control.

It's also imperative to organize your thoughts and get them under control. This will help you be more productive and more discriminating about which thoughts to heed and which to let go of.

Another important thing to assess when you're looking at how you're sabotaging yourself is self-esteem. Self-esteem is a critical tool that directly impacts your performance. It can become a self-perpetuating problem. For example, if you try something and it fails it can reinforce your low self-esteem and there reduce it even more. However, if you have good self-esteem you will also find situations that reinforce your view that you've got this, you are doing well, and can handle what life throws at you.

When you operate from a low self-worth on the left side of the spectrum represented by zero, you're coming from a place of fear. Typically, men fear that they don't measure up and therefore they try to overcompensate. Women often typically have a fear of abandonment. When you operate from fear and a sense of unworthiness, you're constantly seeking reinforcement and approval from the outside world.

On the other side of the spectrum when you have high self-worth, you're operating from a place of love. When you come from a place of love and worthiness, you know that you already have everything that you need inside yourself. Self-confidence that is authentic comes from within and is always coupled with faith. In order to handle the ups and downs of the life and the business world, you always need to be coming from a position of authentic confidence.

I've been in both places. I've seen my sense of worth take a nosedive when things went badly and then watched as I tended to find ways to prove to myself that it was true, I wasn't worth much. The good news is, your brain dug you into that hole and it can dig you out as well. You need to start valuing yourself. Use positive affirmations. At the end of every day, look for things that you did right. When all you can see are the things you did wrong, look for the pieces that were right. Maybe the whole day went sideways but at least you handled it without losing your temper. Focus on what you learned, what you can do different, and praise yourself for handling things as well as you did. Then remind yourself that next time you'll knock it out of the park, no matter what that little annoying voice inside you says.

Shutting Down Your Inner Critic

We all have an inner critic that judges everything we say and do. It's constantly running us down and sowing seeds of doubt, uncertainty, and defeat in our mind. Sometimes it shouts so loud it feels like we don't have any choice but to listen to it. While that inner critic might sound like someone you know, it is all you and is yours to control.

We need to tame the inner voice that criticizes. When you make a mistake that inner critic tells you that you are an idiot. It also loves drama. It loves to show you worst case scenarios and play them all the way through.

It will take you down paths that go something like this: If you don't do this well, you'll lose your job, then you won't be able to pay your mortgage, then your family will be on the streets, and you'll lose everything. Get the idea of "disaster thinking?" We need to tame that inner critic before it becomes a devastating liability.

There are three things you need to do in order to control that inner critic. First, you need to address what your critical self is talking about. Get it down to the specifics and remove emotion from it. For example, admit that you didn't make the sale and that it's because you weren't prepared in your presentation and you didn't ask for the order aggressively enough.

Step two would be to pivot to the positive. Yes, I didn't make the sale but going forward I will prepare myself prior to going into the meeting and always make sure that I will ask for the order more aggressively. Pivot from the negative thing to what positive step you can take.

The third step is to actually give that inner voice a name. For example, call him Negative Nelly. Let Negative Nelly do his thing and allow him to have his say. Know that Negative Nelly is coming from a place of fear and is just trying to protect you. To counter Negative Nelly, you can create a positive voice inside you. Give that one a name as well and ask that one for advice, particularly when Negative Nelly is making you crazy.

Learning to Focus and Avoid Distraction

One of the most important things you can do is to learn to master your own mind. It isn't just the feelings of doubt and the negativity of our inner critic that keep us from achieving that which we set out to do. Our own lack of ability to control our thoughts sidelines us time and again.

The world is full of distractions and there are more of them coming all the time. For example, as an entrepreneur, social media can be an incredibly valuable tool. It can also be a source of tremendous distraction and end up being a time thief that keeps us from accomplishing anything meaningful with our day. When using social media for marketing purposes, it's important to be disciplined and keep yourself on task.

Our minds are designed to suck up information like a sponge. They take in everything they can and are constantly on the lookout for new information, new things to see or hear. This heightened ability to be aware of what's happening around us is a fantastic survival tool we've inherited from our distant ancestors. Unfortunately, the modern world provides an overload of information, the vast majority of which is completely useless.

Television, streaming videos, and the Internet are all wonderlands where we can find mindless entertainment, thought-provoking social commentary, games, news, and lots and lots of advertisements. All of these things flood our senses and vie endlessly for our attention. The problem is the vast majority of it is a complete waste of time. It's a way to drown your life away while distracting your brain from realizing that's what you're doing. You see, the mind demands data and as long as it's getting it, it's happy. It's up to us to police ourselves, to make sure that what we're putting in is beneficial. Twenty-four by seven, we have the ability to tune in and zone out when we should be focused instead on zoning in.

You need to keep your mind clear. The mind is your most powerful tool, but it can drive you insane. You've got to give it clear tasks to do and police what you're putting into it as well as what's coming out of it. You need to eliminate "filler" information because it doesn't help you get where you need to go. You need to eliminate negative, destructive thinking because it can paralyze you with fear, indecision, and inaction and ultimately lead you down wrong paths and into making wrong choices. You need to give your mind periods of rest and rejuvenation as well. You see, your mental health will ultimately drive your performance. Everything you see, every product, idea, service, or action that can be conceived starts in the mind. Only a healthy, rested, properly nourished and fed brain can operate at peak efficiency and ensure that your whole being does as well.

"H" ZONE INTERVIEW ADVICE

from R. Anthony - Singer/Songwriter, TV Contestant on The Voice

> **"You are your worst enemy. You are your worst critic. The mind has a way of shutting you down and it has a way of catapulting you as well, too. It's just very important to stay in a positive place, mentally healthy, and have people around to really push you."**
>
> **- R. Anthony**

Local Tampa Bay resident R Anthony took his singing talents to season three of the hit NBC TV show The Voice. His experience and journey was absolutely incredible. He made the cuts all the way to LA to perform his blind audition on TV, in front of a 15 million viewing audience and also in front of the four celebrity judges: Christina Aguilera, Blake Shelton, Adam Levine, and CeeLo. In an amazing turn of events both Christina and CeeLo wanted him on their team.

CHAPTER 20

Learn to Run New Plays

*"Learning is not attained by chance; it must be sought
for with ardor and attended to with diligence."*
—Abigail Adams.

No matter how good you are, no matter your area of expertise, you need to keep growing, learning, and stretching. If you're not growing, then you're shrinking. If you don't challenge yourself, then you can't continue to reach for new heights. So, don't be afraid to keep going for it, trying and learning new things.

Changing Your Perspective

You know that it takes thirty days to break a habit or create a new one. While most of us think about activities like working out, making our phone calls first thing in the morning, or even putting our keys in the same place so we can find them later, this idea encompasses much more than just our physical activity. This also applies to our mental activity.

We get used to thinking the same way, viewing the world through a certain lens. We even label ourselves, our family members and friends, and our clients. We put them into nice, little boxes and then seldom reevaluate who they are as people or even our relationship with them. A lot of us haven't even reevaluated our idea of what success looks like in five, ten, maybe even forty years. Some of us are living that success and haven't bothered to budge since we got here. Others are still striving for this ancient idea they had of what would make them happy. Sure, some goals don't change for people. However, many change drastically.

What did your ten-year-old self think success would look like? A big house, cool job, fancy car, or amazing spouse? There's probably some of that in there, maybe a lot of that. Just stop and think, though. Are you living the life ten-year-old you dreamed about? Why or why not?

If you're not, what changed? Did you change? Did your goals and values change? Or did you just give up somewhere along the way? It's okay if what you thought you wanted out of life changed, but why didn't you start pursuing the new dreams, the new goals?

It's possible your perspective shifted, but you didn't move your goals to shift with it. It's also possible you've achieved all your goals and have never stopped to look to the horizon and figure out "what next?"

We have a tendency to get stuck in ruts, trapped in patterns. You might very well have had a business for a while and the last five years you achieved your goal of making $100,000 a year. There was a time in your life when that was a staggering number. What about now?

Let me take it one step farther. If you can grow and sustain a company at $100,000 a year, you can grow that same company to $1,000,000 a year. It's all a difference of scaling. You just need to shift your perspective. Every time you achieve your goal, it's time to look for the next thing you're aiming for, the next challenge that's going to stretch you and get you to think faster, be smarter, and achieve more. Fifteen years ago, $100,000 might have seemed impossible, and now it's just a regular annual occurrence.

So, what's your new "impossible?" Is it half a million? A million? Time to go for it so that a few years from now that half a million has become the new normal.

Getting into the Zone is about constantly shifting your perspective. What you did to get there last week isn't going to be good enough to get there next month. You need to be constantly growing, pushing the envelope, and changing your perspective regarding what you are capable of.

The Power of Gratitude

Gratitude is important no matter where you are in your life, regardless of if you're at the top of your game or the bottom. It gives you a perspective and a strength to deal with whatever comes your way.

Football is an intense sport with a lot of potential for physical injury and pain. For myself, I experienced a lot of that. Of course, physical pain is one thing. You deal with it. You get physical therapy, your body heals, and you learn to live with it until the day where hopefully you don't have to anymore. Emotional pain can sometimes be harder to deal with.

When I got cut in the NFL, it was devastating. Obviously, I was very disappointed and that bred a lot of resentment. I got stuck in the trap of "If." "If I'd done this." "If I didn't get hurt." And so on. I'd been focusing on football for so long that there was also this tendency to feel like everything had been taken from me. If I wasn't a football player, then who was I? I went through so many emotions and for years I felt like a failure. I got trapped in the pain of that and it kept me from moving forward in other areas of my life.

Then one day, someone sat me down and told me something that changed my perspective, which in turn changed my life. He said, "Hey, listen, Dude. Look at all your years of experiences that you had, all the things you accomplished, all the accolades, the fun, the friendships, and all that you experienced."

I was just like, "Yeah, so?"

He said, "Let me put it in a different perspective here. You had experiences that 99.9% of the population will never have, and here you think of yourself as a failure. Did you realize that there's a million kids that play high school football every year? Only a couple of hundred thousand go on to play college football?"

I realized he was right. And of those only a few thousand got to be starters their senior year and only a small number sign a contract to come onto an NFL team. He told me that out of a million kids on the same journey I was one of only a few who had the opportunity to sign an NFL contract.

He said, "Stop focusing on what you didn't do. Stop focusing on what you didn't accomplish. Focus on gratitude. Have gratitude and appreciation for the journey you had."

He was telling me to focus on what I did accomplish. Then, he blew my mind even further by telling me that every athlete will stop playing the game at some point. I asked him what he meant.

He said, "Every athlete will stop at some point. Some guys stop at peewee football. Some guys stop in high school. Some guys stop in college. Even the pros, at some point, they get too old, the body breaks down, and they stop playing. You're experiencing what everybody does. They stopped. So did you. Don't ever diminish what your experience was. Focus on what you did do, not what you didn't do."

It was life changing. The truth was I wasn't just diminishing that experience. I was diminishing all of them. I would think about a business my partners and I built from nothing to an eighteen million dollar a year business and I'd think we didn't accomplish anything because we hadn't built a billion-dollar Silicon Valley tech company. I'd think my experiences weren't of value to me and no one could learn from them. You see how self-doubt can mess up your mind and distort your thinking? It's almost comical when you think about it. It's the law of comparison; we constantly are comparing ourselves to the billion-dollar companies, which are not the norm, and falling short. Instead, we don't realize that we've come farther than 99.9% of businesses.

Whether it's business, sports, or your personal life, you need to get out of your head, focus on gratitude, and get a different perspective. Be grateful for the journey and the opportunities you've had. Think about what you've accomplished and not what you haven't. By doing this, you help yourself realize how far you've come, which is a better place to start at when stretching for you next goal. Remember what we talked about with the Zone being a balance of your skill and the challenge presented? Being able to look at where you are realistically helps you to reach for the next challenge that is possible. Focusing on how far short you are compared to others builds within you this unrealistic desire to jump to that and sets you up for failure.

The reality is everybody has experiences. Everybody has a journey. Everybody has lessons they can teach and share with others that can benefit us all because we're all on the same path. We're all trying to accomplish the same things.

It's really important to shift your perspective. It'll help change the story we often tell ourselves, and that story can be limiting, self-imposing. When we shift ourselves, we can take that story and give ourselves a different perspective, and then we can get unstuck. We need to change from what we don't have, and we need to change our perspective to what we do have. Be appreciative and be grateful and use that as a solid foundation to continue your climb.

The Power of Commitment/Conviction

Change is scary. Getting into the Zone isn't a one-time achievement. It's a lifetime pursuit. In order to keep going, you need to have conviction that what you're doing is right. You need to commit to seeing it through. When you commit to doing something, you know in your heart you *have* to do it, it's expected of you by others and yourself. When you have conviction about doing something, you *need* to do it, like you need air. You're not going to able to rest or be comfortable until you've seen it through.

When I had promised *Playboy*, that I would produce and host a one-hour TV special for their Playboy Celebrity Golf Tournament, I didn't truly understand just how far into the deep end I was jumping. I had never done that before. The project seemed doomed to failure so many times. The only thing that kept me going was a deep conviction that it was going to air. That conviction gave me the drive to finish it.

The first part of getting that done was the actual production process. I went out and got a team of cameramen, cohosts, and professional talent who all knew what they were doing to work with me. The lesson here, by the way, is that you can't and shouldn't do everything yourself. That is arguably impossible and certainly crazy.

It was obvious that I was a rookie. My passion, enthusiasm, and commitment to the project were what got those top tier people to work with me. Because of my commitment to the project I was able to negotiate extremely low fees for them to be involved in the project and help me. Of course, the event itself, the Playboy Celebrity Golf Tournament, was a pretty enticing project to begin with.

We got through the shoot in four days. We shot some great footage and got great interviews for the show. When it was all said and done, we had over thirty hours of footage and interviews on tape. My poor editor worked day and night in post-production with me to produce a one-hour TV special on Fox Sports.

Being more experienced today, I could do that off of five hours of tape easily. Back then, though, my attitude was, film and interview anything that moved. I made a lot of mistakes and was very nervous the entire four days of shooting. The important thing was that I faced my fear. I moved through the project and got things done.

During the post-production process, I had some issues getting approval from the corporate headquarters of Fox Sports to air the show. They wanted to approve it before it aired. I was sending them demo segments and they were totally flabbergasted when they realized that I really didn't know what I was doing. One of the guys from Fox Sports took a liking to me and actually turned me over to one of their programmers who helped me review tapes and go back in for numerous reedits. That is totally unheard of. Can you imagine? I was getting on-the-job training from Fox Sports who ended up helping me produce my project to get it ready for TV.

A few times during the process, they told me that it was not going to happen because the show wasn't going to be ready in time. I just continued on with commitment and conviction. I would work for twenty-four hours straight and send them another demo. Time and time again, so many denials were put in front of me. There were so many challenges—so much that said the show wasn't going to happen.

How many times in life do we get beat up with rejection after rejection? You hear "no" continuously and ultimately end up giving up. Thank goodness I had a spirit of conviction because I wouldn't accept "no." It wasn't a possibility, not even an option in my mind.

Finally, two weeks before the air date, Fox Sports gave me the green light. They approved my video. Now the problem was that I needed *Playboy* to review the project and get Hefner to sign off on it.

Playboy told me that this was not going to happen because they needed to have at least a month lead time. Everybody at *Playboy* and Playboy Golf said, "Nice try, but this project is dead and there will be no airing of the show on TV." They said, "Maybe next year." I remember telling the president of Playboy Golf that I would not be denied carrying this project across the threshold and the show would air on TV. He asked how I was going to do it. I said I would figure this out.

So, what I did is I ended up calling a contact at *Playboy* PR who had helped me get back into the *Playboy* mansion to do a reshoot that I didn't do properly at the live event. Typical rookie mistake! I made that phone call to LA, told him my predicament, and overnighted him a demo tape of the show. I made a decision to cut through corporate channels of communication and go directly to the source. I took a shot and it worked. I got the tape to *Playboy* in LA. It was approved, and the show went on as scheduled on national TV on Fox Sports.

The takeaway here is that so many times you'll hear, "No, it can't be done. It's too late." And a thousand other rejections. When you have committed to a vision and a project you have to fight the naysayers and look for every possible resource around you because the possibilities are endless. Who you become in that process is the true gift. The next level of growth you will experience can never be lost! Sometimes, you just need to jump into a project or opportunity and figure it out as you go.

"H" ZONE INTERVIEW ADVICE

from Nick Friedman - Founder/President of College Hunks Hauling Junk & Moving

> **"You have to remind yourself constantly to be grateful and appreciate what you've been able to accomplish and the people who have helped you get there because if you're always looking up and looking ahead, you forget about how far you've come, you forget about how great it is where you are, and you're always just trying to chase the next level."**
>
> **- Nick Friedman**

Nick Friedman's path to multimillion dollar success centers around junk removal. He co-founded College Hunks Hauling Junk & Moving company, and has grown that company into a dominant national franchise with over 100 franchisees across the country and gross annual revenues over 100 million. Nick has been named among the top 30 entrepreneurs in America under 30 by Inc. Magazine. He has appeared on the Oprah Winfrey Show, ABC's Shark Tank, Bravo's Millionaire Matchmaker, The Pitch, and CNBC's Blue Collar Millionaires, among many others.

POWER TIP #3
PREPARE TO BOUNCE BACK
FROM SETBACKS

Everyone gets knocked down. It happens every once in a while. Sometimes, it happens every single day. Life isn't about never getting hit. Life is about what you do and how you deal when you do get hit.

Every great athlete has off days, the quarterback gets sacked multiple times in one game and he's down and he's hurting. The basketball player goes up for a jump shot and comes down wrong, twisting his knee. The fighter ends up hitting the mat when his opponent lands a crucial punch he didn't manage to block.

What defines a great athlete is their ability to press on despite frustration, surprise, and getting the wind knocked out of them. The great athletes are flat on their back looking up and part of them might want to stay there, but they force themselves to their feet. That's what we have to do in business and every other area of our lives.

Even better, if we address the setback with the proper mindset, we can let it motivate us, instead of letting it immobilize us. We need to let it drive us forward instead of holding us back. When you get injured in life, business, or a relationship, the natural tendency is to pull back, lick our wounds, and approach the next obstacle timidly. Some don't even make it that far. Some take the opportunity to give up altogether. I know at times I have done that. Have you?

We all know someone who has let that punch to the gut sideline them for good. We know someone who just doesn't want to put themselves out there and try to meet someone because they're afraid of getting their heart broken again. We know the business owner who lost everything and is too terrified to try again. We probably even know someone who has overcome a major injury or illness only to live their life timidly, constantly afraid of getting sick again. In these cases, these people have been knocked out by life. It happens, but the important thing is to not let that defeat keep you from getting back in the ring of life again.

Ninety percent of staging a comeback is the willingness to do so. All great heroes, both in the real world and in epic fiction, are defined by the obstacles they overcome, the blows they take and forge forward from.

When you get gut punched, embrace it. Be thankful for it. I know that sounds crazy, but you have to look at it that way. All great business-people and athletes have had setbacks along the journey. That's all part of the game. They wouldn't be great if they didn't overcome adversity. They wouldn't become great if they didn't have setbacks. They wouldn't be great if they didn't control their destiny. That's the reality of the game of business and sports. So, know that you're going to have a setback, but just know that you need to get mentally ready to bounce back from the setback and use that as fuel to go to the next level, to break through, to try something different.

I know no greater story than the God saving transformation of former MLB superstar Darryl Strawberry. During and after a seventeen-year professional baseball career, he was dealing with continual substance abuse that caused havoc in his life. He went to rehab four or five times, wasn't ready to stop, and stayed in denial. He dealt with colon cancer and surgery to remove a kidney. Failed marriages and an eighteen-month prison sentence, after leaving a rehab facility and was missing for three days before found sleeping behind a 7-Eleven. He hit rock bottom numerous times.

Darryl finally surrendered. He says, "I tried everything else, but until I got onto this path of my life and really surrendered to God and started living a real life away from all that stuff, it transformed my whole life and made me the person I am today." Darryl and his wife Tracy are ministers and are now sharing their powerful message of redemption and saving thousands of lives doing so!

Remember the story we talked about earlier about the dog sitting on the nail? Some people would rather suffer the pain of that nail than moving on and getting over it. They wallow in the pain they have while telling themselves that they're just avoiding future pain that might be even worse.

Like the dog, you have to choose to move off the nail. Get back up and keep fighting. We all have adversity, pain that hits us. When it happens, have your mental first aid kit ready to go. Address the issue, refocus on your goals, your larger purpose, and decide which step to make first. Use this pain to springboard forward. Let it be the fuel that lights the fire inside you.

Tony Robbins has been inspiring people for years to achieve more and be more. He says people are motivated by one of two things: pleasure or pain. We respond to the pleasure element of acquiring something. We are also motivated and inspired to move away from pain. Sometimes, you have to learn by going through the fire, experiencing the pain.

When you force yourself to use that as a starting point and not an ending point, then you are working at mastering self-discipline, which is essential to becoming your best self and entering the Zone. Remember: no matter who hurt you, what happened to you, you still have control. You never relinquish control even through a storm. You always have control of your own responses and emotions and the power of deciding where you're going and what you'll do next.

POWER TIP #4
KEEP JOURNALS TO TRACK YOUR MINDSET AND PROGRESS

Time is a funny thing. Something that happened a decade or more ago can seem like just yesterday. On the other hand, last year can seem like it was a lifetime ago. We live our lives in certain patterns of behavior that we only change with intentional effort. We might have goals and make plans to accomplish them, and yet find that somehow a year has passed and we're no closer to it.

Have you ever started the New Year with a list of goals or even "resolutions" of things you planned to do in the coming year? Have you then had the experience one year later of realizing that not only did you not accomplish any of those goals but that after about mid-February you didn't even really think about them? That's because our habits, our daily activities take precedence in our minds and our schedules. After a long workday, dinner, and some time spent with family that hour or two you have to yourself somehow becomes vegging out in front of the TV time instead of working on your goals together. Even worse, if you and your spouse or significant other are both vegging out in front of the TV, you think you can justify the wasted time, because it is time spent together.

That's total crap. Unless your current or desired job has something to do with writing or critiquing TV shows, then what you're doing is wasting time, both yours and your spouse's. If you want to spend time together, that's totally fair and a good use of time. Pick an activity that forces you to actively engage with each other, focus on each other instead of the moving images in front of you. Take a walk together, start an active hobby, discuss your plans for the future, or take the time to check in with each other in more than the superficial way you do when you walk through the door. If you want to watch something together, fine, but be intentional about what, when, and how. Maybe instead of just staring at whatever's on, go out to dinner and the movies and make it a proper date night.

The point is, life slips past us incredibly fast and there are a million reasons at the end of the year why we didn't accomplish whatever it was we wanted to. We need to find a way to be more intentional about every aspect of our life, how we spend our time, the things we pursue. A goal that we never progress toward isn't really a goal at all, it's a daydream that we lie to ourselves about to make ourselves feel better.

One of the best ways that we can keep ourselves honest about the effort we're putting forward and on track to our goals is to keep journals. You need to write down what you're trying to accomplish and why. Then, each day, or bare minimum once a week, write down what you did, what you didn't do, and what you need to change about how you're approaching things. Doing it daily is better if you can swing it because it really forces you to become aware of what you actually spend your time on.

These journals are also a great place to keep track of your thoughts and feelings. In order to achieve goals, we need to be clear about what the purpose, the emotion or experience we're hoping to get from the journey is. If you find that you're making steady progress but that you're not enjoying the journey or that you find yourself questioning if the goal is what you actually want, then that is important information. It can help you change course in a timely manner.

It's okay if goals change. It's okay if life is more complicated and things take longer to accomplish. What's not okay is to let time slip by without either pursuing your goals or realizing that you need to swap them out for new goals.

Five minutes a day spent journaling helps you stay on task and get clear about what you're doing, why you're doing it, and even whether you should continue on the path that you're on, make a slight course alteration, or abandon it for another path altogether.

You can do this with every area of your life that you have goals in or need clarity about. It can help keep you intentional and focused on making meaningful connections with family members, friends, and colleagues. It can help you improve your golf game because it can help you identify patterns that you can then get help correcting or strengthening. If you've got a marketing campaign you're rolling out, keep notes about what you do, when you do it, and what the response is. By reviewing these later, it will help you understand how to better reach your target audience and identify potential audiences you hadn't even thought about.

The important thing is to touch base with yourself. Check in and let yourself know what you've done and how you're feeling. Review every month or so to see if there are any things that you can tell need to be adjusted when you see the patterns that are emerging.

POWER TIP #5
VISUALIZE THE DESIRED RESULT

Many people have written on the importance of visualizing your desired result. You might have heard of concepts such as vision boards and focused meditation. When we talked earlier in this book about the characteristics of the Zone, we talked about the importance of focusing on what you want to happen and not what you're afraid could happen. Remember, I dropped the football in what should have been an easy catch because I was telling myself not to drop it? In my head I was caught up in the wrong thought, the wrong image. Then, when I focused on the right thing, catching the ball, I caught a ball in nearly impossible circumstances.

When you're in the Zone, you know what you have to do, and you can see everything playing out exactly as you want it. When trying to work on yourself and get to that peak performance, you need to practice seeing what you want to happen. As a football player, I spent a lot of time both on and off the field visualizing myself in the end-zone catching the football.

Your mind doesn't know the difference between what's real and what you are imagining. So, the idea is that if you fixate on picturing what it is that you want, you move mind and body closer to making it a reality. There's physical practice and then there's mental practice and they're equally important. You have to be mentally ready for the opportunities, obstacles, and big moments that come your way.

For each of your goals, spend a couple of minutes each day visualizing the results. Don't just picture how something will look. Focus also on how it will sound. Which other senses can you get involved in imagining it? How will it feel mentally and emotionally? What will you do in that moment and what will you do later that day to celebrate it?

Getting a strong mental picture of something in your mind helps you stay focused on achieving it. This way when the struggle becomes hard or setbacks threaten your progress you can think about what you want, how it's going to look and feel to get it, and it will give you the strength and the courage to keep pushing forward.

DEFINING WHAT *YOUR* GAME LOOKS LIKE

"Very little is needed to make a happy life; it's all within yourself, in your way of thinking."
—Marcus Aurelius

With the entrepreneurial life, get ready for an incredible ride. If you're an existing entrepreneur, it's time to take a step back and refresh your thinking, refresh yourself, and maybe change some things that you're doing. Get out of the pattern that you seem to be locked in. If you're contemplating becoming a new entrepreneur, there's no better time than today. If you're a former entrepreneur and maybe you're getting bored in retirement, there's no better time to get back in the game than right now.

The important thing to remember is, whatever you want to do, it's *your* game. No one else can choose what game you play or how you play it. The motivation, the desire has to all spring from within you. Everything that you are and everything you've experienced in life are what you bring to the table. They make you unique and your journey will be unique as well. It's important to focus on what you want and why you want it.

CHAPTER 21

Embrace Your Own Game

"Whatever the mind can conceive and believe it can achieve."
—Napoleon Hill

You have to play your own game. You also have to get used to what that entails. It won't be easy, but it will be worth it so long as you're doing it for the right reasons. You have to have a clear vision of what it is you want and go for it.

You Need to Get Comfortable, With Being Uncomfortable

I always stress to people and to companies, you need to get comfortable being uncomfortable. Striving for excellence is not for the faint of heart. You're going to be tested, you're going to be challenged, but that's the game we play. You need to make sure you have a strong commitment to what you're doing and a strong stomach. You need to be ready when the storm hits because the storm is going to hit. You need to be prepared. You need to endure the challenge of that storm. When you get to the other side, once you've been tested, you're going to be stronger and better, and you're going to love the person you become during that process of struggles. It's all about the journey. Life begins at the end of your comfort zone, so make sure you make today uncomfortable. When you're pushed to the limit, when you think you have no more to give, that is when your growth and realization of what your dreams are will come to fruition.

It's Your Game, Not Others'

Getting into the Zone, whether it's in sports, business, or any other area of your life is a very personal experience. You can't compare yourself to others. They are playing their game and you need to be playing yours. So many times, we get caught up in playing someone else's game. Many of us have expectations put on us by parents, teachers, colleagues, and even significant others. They want us to do this or that with our life. Of course, the cliché is that parents are always hoping their kid grows up to be a doctor or lawyer. Some parents might push you to take over the family business.

The thing is, this is your life, and no one can live it but you. It might be scary to take responsibility for your own life and decisions. On some level, it can be comfortable to just live up to other's expectations of us. We think it will eliminate the hard conversations that happen when you say things like "I don't want to take over the family business" or "I want to be a painter, not a doctor." Look, you didn't choose your parents' life for them. And, in the same way, when the time comes you should let your kids choose their path instead of forcing them into yours. You are a unique individual with your own gifts, skills, and passions. You need to chase your dreams and not give into others' expectations of who you are or what you're "supposed" to be.

When you do pick your path, make sure that you don't get caught in a very different but equally dangerous trap of trying to live someone else's journey. What others have done before you can also become a point of obsession. We are constantly comparing ourselves to other people. This is a phenomenon that starts when we are little. Well-meaning adults compared us to this or that relative in how we looked, how we acted, our personality, and our abilities, all of it. It's only natural that as we grow, we compare ourselves to other people.

It's important to remember that just as no two people are the same, no two journeys are the same. You might want to be a professional basketball player and if you have the skill and the drive you can achieve that. Don't expect your journey to be just like Michael Jordan's, though. His journey was his own. If it takes you longer or you never do the exact same things or win as many games don't let yourself get hung up on that. The only person you should be comparing yourself to is your past self. Are you better than you were yesterday? What are you doing today so that tomorrow's self will be better than you are today?

Some people graduate law school with perfect GPAs. Others struggle to get it done with grades that are barely passing. One takes the Bar Exam and passes on the first try. Another doesn't pass until the fifth try. At the end of the day they're both attorneys even if their paths looked very different from each other. Set your expectations based on you and your journey and not someone else. Getting into the Zone is about achieving your personal best, not playing down to someone not as good as you nor vainly striving to play as well as someone twice as good as you.

You're Never Too Old; You're Never Too Young

Don't let your age discourage you and don't let anyone else's opinion on the matter dissuade you. There are high schoolers who start businesses and become millionaires before they're old enough to vote. There are retirees who decide to do something new and succeed beyond wildest expectations. Grandma Moses didn't pick up a paintbrush until she was in her 70s and went on to be a celebrated and prolific painter.

Nick Friedman and his partner created College Hunks Hauling Junk while they were in college. After college, they tried working corporate jobs and after six months quit to work full time on the business they had created. They quickly expanded and franchised out. They've received a lot of attention for building so much while they were under thirty.

Of course, you don't have to be young to start up a business and grow it into a huge success. You're never too old. Whether you're 20 or 70, there are opportunities for you to take advantage of and have the best time of your life.

Rhonda Shear is a fantastic example of someone who reinvented her life and started an entirely new business when she was in her 40s. She's in her 60s now and is going stronger than ever, growing her business and living her best life. She started with nothing and built an 80 million dollar a year company with her husband.

Julie Weintraub, the Founder and CEO of Hands Across the Bay charity, an organization that helps domestic violence victims and those who are in need in the Tampa Bay area, started her charity based on a desire to have accountability on where gifted dollars went. She and her husband Steve, were frustrated when they learned that a good percentage of charitable donations, get eaten up in an organization's operating costs. That fueled their burning desire to have full transparency and get more dollars to help victims. That was over ten years ago, and today, Hands Across the Bay is has become a shining light in touching so many lives in the Tampa Bay community.

It also doesn't matter how many businesses you've tried and failed at. You don't know what's going to hit big. So, bring something into the marketplace and if it fails, then try something else. If it succeeds, then build on your success, one step at a time. Regardless of your age and experience, adversity will always be there but so will opportunity.

"H" ZONE INTERVIEW ADVICE

from Kato Kaelin - Actor, Radio and Television Personality, Businessman

"I know we're on this earth [a] very short time. I always [say] we're on earth for a semester. You got to have fun. And I think I do live for fun, and that's true. But that doesn't mean I'm a partier. It means I love life, and I really, really embrace life."
- Kato Kaelin

Kato Kaelin gained international fame as a witness in the O.J. Simpson murder trial. Kaelin is an actor and television personality. He started his own company selling loungewear.

CHAPTER 22

Wheel of Life

Life is a series of tiny miracles. Notice them.

One of the secrets of success is finding a way to achieve balance in your life. There can be a temptation to focus solely on your work and ignore other aspects of your life. That might work for a short while, but eventually you will burn out or the other areas of your life will come crashing down and demand attention from you.

Think about your health, for example. Say you're really hustling. You burn the midnight oil and you routinely put in twelve to sixteen-hour days or more trying to achieve as much as you possibly can. In order to do that you're most likely shortchanging other areas of your life. People like to make jokes like, "I'll sleep when I'm dead." Meanwhile, they'll just keep pushing their body harder and harder. Oftentimes, exercise and healthy eating end up eventually going out the window, too.

Sooner or later if you don't take care of your body, if you don't focus on your health, your body will force you to stop everything else and focus on it. You'll get rundown and you'll end up getting sick. Your body might start off trying to get your attention with decreased ability to fight off colds, but believe me, it can only escalate from there. It will usually pick the worst possible time to breakdown. When your health is not working, it doesn't matter what's going on with the other parts of the wheel of life and it will most certainly have a negative impact on your ability to do your job.

Even if you eat right, exercise, and get enough sleep, you still need to factor in serious downtime. Just as your body needs to rest and be taken care of, so does your mind. Without downtime, relaxation, and time spent with friends and family, stress just builds and builds. When you don't have an outlet for releasing that stress it will start to impact your work performance and your physical health. Mind and body love to work together that way. When one's out of alignment, they both are. That's because they're just two spokes on what I like to call the Wheel of Life.

The Wheel of Life is just that. It's your life and the various components that it's made up of. Work, health, and family all help make that wheel go round. A wheel is so successful. A wheel can work because it's evenly balanced, and it's able to keep turning in a never-ending motion because it's got a structure around it. If you divide up your life and the things you spend time and energy on, you can divide it into some different components that make up this wheel.

You have a health and fitness component. You have a family and relationships component. Your career and your business are other components of who you are. Your financial well-being is a separate component because you can make millions, but managing your money is a separate issue. Then, you have your personal growth, your personal development. Then, you could have your spirituality. All those comprise the different components of the Wheel of Life.

You've got to look at your life as a complete game plan. Your life has so many consistent, variable pieces to it. It's not enough to focus on just one aspect. It's also not enough to just have a plan for one or even two areas of your life. To be balanced, you have to address each area. You're not just an entrepreneur, that's just one aspect of your life.

I challenge you to take some quiet time, get away from all the noise that's out there. There are a thousand distractions trying to eat up your time. You need to get quiet and spend time going through your wheel of life. On a scale of 1 to 10, with 10 being the highest level of maxed out enjoyment or fulfillment, rate the different areas of your life.

Determine what your potential is. Are you honoring your God-given ability that's instilled in you to be able to go to the next level? Ask yourself some questions. If you knew you couldn't fail, what are some things you would want to accomplish in each of these areas? What are some things you want to experience in those areas of life? Essentially, we have to figure out what are we looking for. We have goals, but what are we looking for?

We're looking for the experience behind the goal. For example, I want to lose 20 pounds. Do I really want to lose 20 pounds, or do I want to have the experience of what it feels like when your suit fits properly? At the end of the day, it's the experience, the feeling, we really want, not just achieving the goal.

I challenge you to identify your wheel of life. What makes you tick? Become aware. Sometimes, we have a distorted perspective and we tell ourselves certain things based on conditioning or expectations (ours or other people's). We need to shift our thinking, get back to a baseline. Where am I? What am I doing? What's left inside me? Those are the things that are really important because, if you look at it, you're spending a third of your life, in essence, sleeping. You're spending a third of your life in your business, in your career. You're spending a chunk eating and just taking care of basic daily functions. That doesn't leave a lot of time left and we need to be intentional with that time if we hope to achieve any of the things we want or have the experiences we're craving.

So, just like you go to the doctor every so often for a checkup, it's time to do a life checkup. Where are you at? Where do you want to be? How are you going to get there? It's time to do an assessment.

Now, think about your ideal in each of these areas. If you knew you could not fail, what would you attempt? It's important to have clarity about this so that you know what it is you're striving for. What would happen in your career? What type of business would you be involved in? What about your health, your wellness, your family? What would you see happen? Where would you live? What would you want to learn? What attributes do you want to acquire? Where do you want to improve on those things?

In each of these areas of your life, you can strive for the Zone. You don't want to just perform your best at work but also in your relationships, in your well-being, and in your life in general. When we are striving to improve in all these key areas, then we are bettering our lives in every way possible and making it so that when we are in the Zone the gains will be even that much more obvious. We are also ensuring that our relationships or our health aren't being sacrificed to our business interests.

"H" ZONE INTERVIEW ADVICE

from Nick Friedman - Founder/President of College Hunks Hauling Junk & Moving

"I try to put my phone away when I'm home. I try to be present mentally, not just physically, when I'm at home with the family, and I think that is really important because you can burn yourself out if all your focus is on one single thing, and it is very difficult to achieve sort of this work/life balance. So, you have to constantly discipline yourself to do that."

- Nick Friedman

Nick Friedman's path to multimillion dollar success centers around junk removal. He co-founded College Hunks Hauling Junk & Moving company, and has grown that company into a dominant national franchise with over 100 franchisees across the country and gross annual revenues over 100 million. Nick has been named among the top 30 entrepreneurs in America under 30 by Inc. Magazine. He has appeared on the Oprah Winfrey Show, ABC's Shark Tank, Bravo's Millionaire Matchmaker, The Pitch, and CNBC's Blue Collar Millionaires, among many others.

CHAPTER 23

Seeing the End-Zone

"There are two great days in a person's life, the day
we are born and the day we discover why."
—*Mark Twain*

It's important to keep your eye on the prize. That's something we hear a lot. It's an admonition not to get so wrapped up in minutiae or distracted by other things that you lose focus, lose your momentum, and forget where you are going. You need to have a clear vision of what it is you're attempting to do, where you're going, and why. Otherwise, how do you know when you get there?

Goals and the Experience and Feelings behind the Goals

It's not enough to just have a goal. If you want to achieve your goals, you need to attach feelings to them. You want to be able to close your eyes and know what the experience will mean to you. How will it make you feel when you achieve it? The more you can visualize, the better it is. Attach as many of your senses to it as possible.

Like with your goals in general, this is highly personalized. No one can tell you why you want these goals except you. Don't try to create feelings and reasons based on what other people say they've done. This is your Zone that you're trying to reach. Everything about the journey has to be tailored to you in order to take advantage of your uniqueness as a person. Why does this journey mean so much to you? What do you hope to gain from it? What experience do you think it will provide you? The more focused and clear you can be in your answers the more determined your mind will be to get you there.

Evaluating Your Progress

So, step one is assess the gap, the difference between where you are and where you'd like to be. You need to have the courage to be brutally honest with yourself on this. Step two: start working on it now; don't procrastinate. Step three: assess and monitor. Figure out what you're doing on a daily, weekly, and monthly basis. Step four: make adjustments as things progress. Don't wait until the end of the year. It's like sailing, when the wind shifts, you have to make adjustments to your sails as you're going along.

You need to constantly evaluate your progress. This means that ideally you need a concrete, defined way to do so. As a football team marches down the field each yard gained moves them toward their goal. They all can tell how close they are and how much further they have to go before they hit the end-zone.

If you don't have clear objectives and check in to see how you're progressing, how will you ever know when you make it to the goal? Check-ins also help provide momentum. As you see yourself progressing it gives you the strength and mental fortitude to keep pressing forward even when it's hard, even when you're tired.

When you evaluate your progress you also have an opportunity to discover exactly what's working and what's not working. It's like when you run a marketing campaign. If you spend $1,000 in ad money in one place and gain 10 prospects from that ad that's a 1% return. If you're evaluating your progress, though, you have a chance to discover that $100 spent elsewhere gets you 10 prospects as well. That's a 10% return and it tells you that you should be spending more money in that area because it will get you to your goal either faster or cheaper (or a combination of the two).

Evaluating your progress is also a great way to figure out where you might be losing time or productivity. Maybe you'll discover that no matter what you do, on Friday afternoons your team just can't focus. That tells you that it might be time to try a new tactic or incentive to keep them on task through the end of the work week. It at least tells you not to schedule crucial meetings during that time because you won't be likely to get the best result.

You might discover that you are somehow able to get through your call sheet faster if you do it first thing in the morning than if you do it early afternoon. That kind of information is invaluable. It will help you be more efficient and productive.

Evaluating once isn't enough. It needs to be an ongoing process. As you grow, as you move through life and progress toward some goals, achieve others, or even realize you need to change some you need to give yourself the opportunity to adapt. You need to be able to shed your skin to keep evolving, keep growing.

There are many ways we can help ourselves through this process. Planning, strategizing, goal setting, writing down our intentions on paper, rereading them frequently, taking quiet time to talk or think about it. These are important.

So, how far out should you be planning for any given chunk of time? Before you get there. A lot of people plan their lives based on a calendar year, starting on January 1st. That's great. I certainly do that. However, I don't wait until January 1st to start planning. I want to be able to hit the ground running. So, I start planning the year in mid-November. I'm making changes and then as I go into January I'm already in stride with the new, I'm already in flow.

Let me tell you a secret. A lot of companies don't bother trying to do business toward the end of the year. That's a mistake. They reason that because it's the holidays and everyone's taking off on vacation, there's no use in bothering. People and businesses get in the mindset of "No one's buying my product or my service. No one's around in the marketplace." With that kind of thinking, we define our outcome already. And a lot of times there are people that are doing business or making some things happen all the way through the holidays and the New Year.

My point is that when you're able to flow and manage your expectations, see what's going on, what you have, what you want to do, what changes you want to have, you can head into the New Year in full stride. I like that advanced preparation because it means you don't lose or waste time like almost everyone else. Imagine if you weren't prepared before January. You were at a New Year's Eve party and then on January 1st you're just kind of recovering and watching football games. On January 2nd, you're sluggish and trying to regroup from all the holidays, realizing that you've put on a few pounds in the last month and everything is out of step. By January 3rd, you're trying to get back to work. You try to get organized. You spend a bunch of time reshuffling and thinking, and it's not until somewhere around January 15th that you start getting into a flow that works. If that's the outcome you want, fine. Shut it down and regroup in the middle of January.

But know that there are other people, like me, who are going to be on it. I like to have my flow going on January 1st so I start the New Year fresh and in high gear. It makes me feel good. Then I take my targeted time during the course of the year to recharge, to regroup, and then every day I get back to it.

I'm taking care of myself every day with my health, my family time, and work and try to balance things better at this stage of the game in my life than I did at the earlier stage of the game of my life. Every day is that gift.

The way you plan out your year should also be the way you plan things out in smaller chunks. Remember, you look at your overall defined outcome and work backward to see what steps have to be taken when to achieve it. For me, every day is almost like a mini year. The beginning of the day is the New Year. The midday is midyear. The end of the day, the evening, is wrapping the year up, getting ready for the new day tomorrow.

Let's say that you're a business owner and your business is currently bringing in $600,000 a year and after expenses the profit is $100,000. Now, maybe you decide you'd rather bring in $1,000,000. That sounds great, but work through it. If you put in all the time and money to make the $1,000,000 but after expenses your profit is only $50,000, then what was the point? Were you better off generating less revenue income with a higher profit margin?

Whatever your end goal is, take it and work backward to see how you get there. What do you have to accomplish semi-annually, quarterly, monthly, and daily to make it happen? If you need so many customers, how many prospects does that take? How many leads turn into prospects? How many calls turn into leads? Once you can work backward, you have a map to get where you are going and you know what the daily, monthly, and quarterly tasks and steps have to be. The more you can quantify something, the easier it will be to know if you're on track to achieve your goals.

When Goals Change

Sometimes in life, our goals change and that's okay. Sometimes something comes along that changes the course of your life or the trajectory of your business. Sometimes these things hit us out of the blue. It could be that you're suddenly expecting a new baby right as your other child is getting ready to start college. As in my case, that certainly shifts your thinking about the future, let me tell you! It could be that technology or the market changes in a way that makes your old goals or business obsolete. While that can be frustrating, you need to learn to go with the flow, pivot to the new. Or it might simply be that something changed inside of you. Perhaps you discovered a new passion or realized that what you thought you wanted is not going to make you happy like you assumed it would

Whatever the reason, when goals change it's important to adapt and go with it. Reevaluate what it is you want. Remember to attach the emotions to the new goals just like you did with the original ones. Don't waste time wallowing in self-pity if you feel the decision was thrust upon you. Don't beat yourself up over what happened in the past and what you might have done differently. Focus on the future and how you're going to make it glorious.

When you've had defined goals that you've been working toward, changing course can be harder than if you had no goals to begin with. That's okay. It's also okay to take a step back and breathe while you reassess what the new course of action is going to be. The ability to adapt is a sign of intelligence. It's also a crucial skill to surviving in the world of business where done deals can fall apart overnight and unexpected opportunities can grab hold of you and refuse to let go.

A quarterback has a plan when he's going to run a play. He communicates the plan to his team. He knows who's going to be where and who he intends to throw the ball to. Once the snap happens and the ball is in play, though, things can change rapidly. Great quarterbacks can adapt. If their intended receiver just can't get in the clear, they are able to quickly evaluate who else to get the ball to. Sometimes, they end up running it themselves. The point is, when circumstances change or are not what you expected them to be, it's wasted effort to follow through on the existing plan, knowing it's doomed to failure. Successful athletes know that in the moment, things change. In order to be successful, they have to be willing and able to change, too.

When your goals change, whether by necessity or free will, make sure to change everything else accordingly. If you have a vision board or affirmations, update them to reflect the new goal. Be clear with yourself why the goal has changed and attach intense emotions to the new goal in order to help you stay on task even when you're asking yourself why.

You Constantly Need to Reinvent Yourself

"Good enough" is almost never good enough in any aspect of life. The hard part is that the thing that you're trying to tell yourself is "good enough" might well be yesterday's "great." Unfortunately, life doesn't stay static. When you achieve a new goal, a new level in business or in life, that becomes your new normal. In order to excel you have to fix your sights on the next thing.

In order to do that, you need to work on improving yourself including your skills and your mindset. The world and the marketplace are continuously growing, evolving, adapting. If you don't evolve and adapt, you'll find yourself out in the cold.

Think about it this way. Let's say you started playing football when you were a kid. You were in Pop Warner or played pickup games with your friends in the street. Imagine you got really good at it so that you were one of the best players you knew. That's great, but that's a really small segment of society you're competing against. You're also a kid, playing with a kid's level of coordination, skill, speed, and strength. You also have a kid's understanding of strategy and you'll probably find you and your friends have a certain limited pool of plays.

You grow up and you try out for football in high school. Maybe you're lucky and the coach takes a chance on you. You're suddenly playing against guys who are Juniors and Seniors. Your "A" game is their "C" game. You adapt. Your body is also changing. You're getting taller, bigger. You can hit harder and run faster. The coach trains you on more plays. By the time you're an upperclassman your "A" game is so far above and beyond what it was two or three years earlier.

You get on the college football team and everything repeats. You pack on more muscle, more bulk. You have more control over your body. Your mind is also starting to play catchup and you start to understand technique, strategy, and subtlety far more. You learn even more about how to be a great team player, working in tandem with the other guys to get the job done. By the time you get your shot at playing professionally, you have very little in common physically, mentally, and emotionally with the ten-year-old version of you. You grew, evolved, and stepped up into each new challenge of the game. You transformed yourself and your game. If at any point in your journey you had decided that your game was "good enough" you never would have progressed to the next level. Your career would have ended in Pop Warner or high school or college.

Sometimes reinventing yourself means more than just stepping up your game. Sometimes you need to literally scrap everything that's come before and start fresh. A new career, a new relationship, even a new home-town can be both exciting and frightening. If you're lucky and clever, you'll find ways to utilize some of your old skills in your new world.

Entrepreneur Rhonda Shear did just that. She had a prolific film and television career and was the host of the popular *Up All Night*. Eventually, the acting jobs started to dry up and she knew she needed to do something new. Newly married with no money and no prospects, she came up with a new idea. She went on the Home Shopping Network and tried her hand being a celebrity endorser, promoting intimate apparel that she liked.

Using her skills as an actress and her experience as a television host, she went on and sold out within the first couple of minutes. Just like that she pivoted from being an actress to being a businesswoman specializing in women's intimates.

She and her husband partnered with a small company that was also trying to really get going to produce a line of clothing for her. The "Ahh Bra" was born and Rhonda became a force to be reckoned with.

You might think it was easy for her because she was a celebrity. Not true. She and her husband were both broke and couldn't get loans from banks or even friends to help them. Larger manufacturers turned them down because they wanted financial guarantees that Rhonda just couldn't provide at that time. It was through hustle, foresight, and tenacity that she finally found a manufacturer who would work with her and she fought tooth and nail to make things happen.

Business mogul was a second career for Rhonda and she arguably has been even more successful with it than her first one. She had to be willing to work hard and reinvent herself to get to the top, though. Sometimes life demands that you start over. When it does, you need to rise to the challenge like Rhonda did.

"H" ZONE INTERVIEW ADVICE

from R. Anthony - Singer/Songwriter, TV Contestant on The Voice

> **"I'd say this is how you know it's a dream, when it doesn't let you go. Many times I wanted to throw singing away. I wanted to stop, because things just weren't panning out. I wanted to quit, but it never let me go. Every morning I wake up and it's holding on to me."**
>
> **- R. Anthony**

Local Tampa Bay resident R Anthony took his singing talents to season three of the hit NBC TV show The Voice. His experience and journey was absolutely incredible. He made the cuts all the way to LA to perform his blind audition on TV, in front of a 15 million viewing audience and also in front of the four celebrity judges: Christina Aguilera, Blake Shelton, Adam Levine, and CeeLo. In an amazing turn of events both Christina and CeeLo wanted him on their team.

POWER TIP #6
LOVE WHAT YOU ARE DOING

Choose a job you love, and you'll never have to work a day in your life.

You need to love what you're doing. It might seem like an obvious thing, but it's amazing how many things we chase after in life because we feel like we have to. It might be an obligation or someone else's dream, such as a parent or spouse. At the end of the day, though, you are the one who has to be excited about what you're doing if you ever hope to achieve your best.

A lot of times, people have this vision of starting their own business, being an entrepreneur, or going into sales. They want to be successful and make a lot of money. The reality, though, is that it's not about being on the cover of *Entrepreneur* magazine and having a billion-dollar tech company overnight, if ever. The reality is that you build a business over time. You're going to walk through dark valleys that test your faith in yourself, your company, your product, everything.

When you go through those dark valleys, if you don't have a passion, a deep love, for what you're doing then you're not going to make it out the other side. When the obstacles come, when you get punched in the gut, you're going to decide it's not worth it and give up. So, if you're doing something for someone else, or a job you feel obligated to do or have been told to do, make an assessment of where you are, where you're going, and why. Ask yourself what you want to do and then make sure you go on that journey instead. You spend a third of your life working at a job or a career. It needs to be worth it. When someone asks you why you're doing what you're doing, the answer needs to be, "Because I love it." Otherwise, there are other things you could and should be doing.

Life is short. You blink your eyes and the game will-end, time will have run out. We want to spend our time enjoying and loving what we're doing. Even then, you're going to get beat up, have those obstacles that get in your way. It's the passion that will carry you through all that. Otherwise you risk ending up burned out, bitter, and having lived someone else's idea of your life and not yours.

My oldest daughter, Alexis, is amazing. When she has something she wants to do, that she's passionate about, she can't stop talking about it. She'll have endless amounts of energy and she'll make things happen. She'll get up at 2 a.m. just to do whatever she needs to do to make it happen. That's because that fire carries her through any adversity.

When you don't have that passion, everything can become a drag. Your energy might be low and whatever fire might be burning inside you is easily diminished. You need to have passion to keep that flame of action and intention alive. With that love you can weather the worst storms and the adventure that is being an entrepreneur.

POWER TIP #7
CREATE YOUR ENVIRONMENT

*The five people that you're hanging with most are
going to dictate your future success.*

It's important to create an environment conducive to success. Organizing your physical environment in a certain way will make you more efficient. It can even impact your mood and make for greater productivity. Beyond the physical aspects of your environment, you also need to be thinking of the people around you in those environments. They will also impact your productivity and mood for better or worse.

Hang with the Eagles

Many people in this world are toxic. Chances are you know several like that. They might be family, friends, coworkers, etc. The problem is, those people drag you down and get you focused on negativity. What you feed your brain is what it puts out. If you're trying to improve yourself, to do better, and achieve more, you can't afford to fill your brain with constant negative chatter and the pessimism of others.

Some of these people might think of themselves and put themselves forward as "helpful" because they're good at pointing out obstacles before you crash headfirst into them. Only problem is, they're so fixated on obstacles that they never see opportunities. And, as we've seen earlier, what you focus on tends to be what actually happens. Focus on not wanting to drop the ball and you end up dropping the ball because in your mind the image of dropping it was too strong. You can't soar with the eagles if you're stuck on the ground being pecked to death by the chickens.

They say that the five people you are hanging around most dictate your level of success. Hang around a bunch of negative people who put in minimum effort for minimum reward and that's where you'll be stuck. Hang around a bunch of positive people who work hard, play hard, and achieve the maximum reward and they'll elevate you to your level. You'll naturally begin to do the same kinds of things and model the same kind of attitude and work ethic.

As part of the people you surround yourself with, you'll want to find a mentor or coach. Actually, you'll probably want to find more than one, but starting with one is good. Self-awareness is an important part of the journey. And having a team with a coach or mentor you can talk to and bounce ideas off of is crucial. They can help you understand the journey you're on. They'll look at your challenges from a slightly different perspective and help you come up with solutions you might not have thought of.

You can get training, mentorships, explore new skillsets, and find someone to coach you or just sit down and have lunch with you. Find someone who inspires you, one you can learn from, and offer to buy them lunch. Tell them why they inspire you and most people are happy to talk and give you advice and insight. These are all things you can do that keep propelling you forward while you're trying to keep moving to the bigger purpose of what you're trying to accomplish. Mentors can help you shave time off of learning curves and help you while you're struggling for that breakthrough.

You need to find people who will challenge you, hold you accountable, and push you to that higher level. You need to be able to trust them through the process. They have to believe in you 100% or they can't help you. This can be hard because there are people in our lives, often family or longtime friends, who we think believe in us. Oftentimes, some of these people turn out to be dream hackers who don't want us to ascend to the next level. They want to keep us right where we are, on their level. If we achieve, then it challenges their comfort zone and the status quo of their lives and the relationship. This is one of the reasons you should be cautious about whom you share your dreams with. You want to share them with people who will push you to achieve them, not people who will hold you back.

Create Routines

In creating an environment, it's important to create a routine. This includes proper exercise and nutrition. To reach peak performance, you have to be in your best shape mentally and physically. We get there through consistent, dedicated work. One of the things you need to ask yourself about the different habits and routines you have in your life is: *Does this routine help me and can I change it in some way to take me to the next level?*

When taking away an old habit, it's crucial to add a new one in to replace it. Sometimes, change is uncomfortable. That influx of a new thing creates a game change and pushes you outside your comfort zone. You know what? Appreciate that. Feel the discomfort, let it move inside you. Let it move through you. Breathe and remind yourself that there have been times in the past when you've tried something new and it's created new experiences and opportunities. Open your mind up.

When trying new things, you have to give it time to unfold and work for you. This includes changes to your environment and new people you're hanging with. Add in one or two new, positive people while slowly spending less time with the people that are dragging you down. Notice the difference it eventually makes in the way you think, feel, talk, and act. Give yourself time to go through the process.

POWER TIP #8
ALWAYS CHALLENGE YOURSELF

Don't rest on your laurels. That's something you hear, particularly after you've achieved something in your field. Attaining a goal isn't a once-in-a-lifetime thing. Think about football. You won a game. That's fantastic! However, that doesn't make you a star for life. Far from it. You won one game in an entire season. Next week, there's another game. If you fumble the ball and cost your team the victory, what you did the week before will soon be forgotten, or, at least, diminished by your most recent showing. When dealing with clients it's the same thing. You might have made them or saved them a lot of money last year. That victory only lasts so long before they're looking at you and asking, "What have you done for me lately?"

You always have to challenge yourself. It's not going to ever get to the point where it's easy, it's automatic. You always have to keep growing. That means getting training if you need to be better at sales or trying new approaches when it comes to marketing. You have to adapt and embrace new technologies and new platforms. Ask yourself what you can do to keep enhancing the business, product, or service. Are there joint partnerships or joint ventures you can form?

The minute you say "I have arrived," then you're in trouble. You think you've done it all and know it all. If you're not climbing up the mountain then you're sliding down. Growth takes effort. You need to keep pushing the boundaries, including those of your comfort zone. You've got to continually be pushing yourself when it comes to discipline, media marketing, sales, and your own mindset.

When you do something consistently over and over, you have a multiplier effect, like compound interest. Every time you're consistent doing something, you're getting closer to your end result. You need to create positive habits. Constantly challenging yourself to do better is one of them.

PART VI

WHEN YOU'RE IN THE *ZONE*

Make the rest of your life the best of your life.

You've made it! You're in the Zone! That's fantastic. Now is the time to work your hardest, take advantage of every second you're there. The moment you step foot outside the Zone is when you should start planning your return trip.

Those at the top of their game spend a lot of time around the Zone and as much time in it as they possibly can. They also know the secret to refocusing as they leave the mountain and prepping themselves to get back into the Zone as quickly as possible.

CHAPTER 24

Reaching the Zone

"Life is like riding a bicycle, to keep your balance,
you must keep moving forward."
—*Albert Einstein*

When all your hard work, training, and mental discipline finally pay off and you enter the Zone, it's a feeling like no other. You'll notice that the things we discussed in Part II happen. Time will either stand still or speed by while you're operating at peak proficiency. Whether you're in the Zone for minutes, hours, or days, take full advantage of the time there.

Take Advantage of It

Football teams spend their entire year trying to hone the skills of individual players and trying to build a cohesive team that elevates all the players to do their best. Everyone wants to have those games, those plays, where they're doing their best work. Arguably, a lot of the culmination of months of hard work is the Super Bowl where hopefully everyone steps up and performs to the best of their abilities.

At the end of the game one team has gotten into the end-zone more than the other and has won. The victory celebration brings with it a lot of special moments and opportunities. There are rings, parades, trips to Disney and the White House that the winning team gets to enjoy. All their hard work earned them those things.

When you're in the Zone, take advantage of every second you can. Don't stop to focus too much on the rewards or accolades people might be throwing your way. Those can be enjoyed and appreciated once you've achieved your goal.

Live every second that you're performing at your top level to its fullest. Then, afterward, enjoy the success that you've achieved. You've earned it. At the very least, make sure to mark the occasion and let yourself focus on all you did accomplish. Don't get caught up in stressing out when you exit the Zone that you're never going to make it back there. Use the whole experience as a boost to your confidence as well as your business and personal life.

Know that It Won't Last

When you're on the top of the mountain, when you're in the Zone, there is no better feeling in the whole world. Everything is breaking your way. You're performing beyond even your expectations of yourself. And the view is breathtaking. However, you can only breathe that rarified air for a short while. Eventually, you come down from the mountain and you step out of the Zone.

The euphoria of those moments and all that you accomplished might linger for a little while. Soon, though, reality is going to come crashing down. You're no longer climbing toward your peak. And that descent can sometimes feel a lot like falling. You might be tempted to beat yourself up and ask yourself why you couldn't stay there one more minute, one more day, one more week. The truth is the Zone is a shifting target.

Even if you could manage to maintain that level indefinitely, it doesn't mean that you're staying in the Zone. It means that you've achieved a new normal and to get back to the Zone you're going to have to push yourself even harder, further, and faster. It only makes sense. After all, as you progress through your career, your chosen sport, your life, you gain wisdom, experience, and skill. Your best efforts today are so much more impressive than your best efforts five, ten, twenty years ago. Remember, you from five or ten years ago would be overjoyed to be at the normal operating level that your current self is.

Life is a competition. While there are plenty of people out there we might be in competition with on some level, who we are truly competing against is ourselves. We are constantly striving to top our own personal best, even when we are at the top of our field and have blown the rest of the competition away. Look at competitive swimmers. Sure, they want to win their race, but they're also fixated on besting themselves. They want to break their own personal record. And if their personal record was already a world record, so much the better.

You can't stay in the Zone indefinitely, but you can take advantage of it while you're there. You can also get ready to get there the next time.

"H" ZONE INTERVIEW ADVICE

from Nick Friedman - Founder/President of College Hunks Hauling Junk & Moving

> **"You've got to have a purpose that drives you more than just making money so that you stay motivated when things do get tight, or when things do get tough."**
>
> **- Nick Friedman**

Nick Friedman's path to multimillion dollar success centers around junk removal. He co-founded College Hunks Hauling Junk & Moving company, and has grown that company into a dominant national franchise with over 100 franchisees across the country and gross annual revenues over 100 million. Nick has been named among the top 30 entrepreneurs in America under 30 by Inc. Magazine. He has appeared on the Oprah Winfrey Show, ABC's Shark Tank, Bravo's Millionaire Matchmaker, The Pitch, and CNBC's Blue Collar Millionaires, among many others.

CHAPTER 25

Preparing for Your Next Shot at the Zone

"If you don't act on life, life will act on you."
—Robin Sharma

You're coming down the mountain. You're stepping out of the Zone. As you're feeling that letdown, taking that descent, don't focus on the bottom. That's not where you want to go. In fact, do what you can to avoid that. Instead, set your eyes on the next challenge, the next peak. The more you set your mind and focus on achieving that next peak the less down time you're likely to have. Top achievers, those who are truly motivated, don't spend all their time in the Zone, but they spend the majority of their time closer to it than other people. They also get there more frequently than other people. That's because they don't focus on the letdown, they focus on the success and use that as a springboard to take on the next, bigger challenge. They have the confidence that since they made it once they can make it again and again.

Confidence is Only Half of it, You Also Need Preparation

Those top performers use the confidence that their successes have given them. They don't just rely on their existing skills and experience, though. They know that confidence will only get them so far. They also need to prepare.

As you set your sight on the next mountain you're going to climb, you need to keep practicing your existing skill set. You also need to spend some time figuring out what new skills and tools you might need to get there. Some of your existing infrastructure, work processes, and personal habits might not be enough to get you to that next peak.

Nick Friedman, President and co-founder of College Hunks Hauling Junk & Moving, recalls one of the problems they ran into when scaling up their business. They had been using out-of-the-box software to handle their scheduling and dispatching. The problem was it didn't function for them as well as it should. Ultimately, as they expanded the business, they ended up having to have custom software designed for them that could do everything they needed it to efficiently and easily.

Nick and his partner achieved a lot of success and hit a lot of peaks with that software that wasn't exactly right for them. There came a day, though, where they knew it was time to upgrade so they could continue to stretch to the next peak, conquer the next mountain.

The same is true with our personal routines and habits. Say you're in amazing shape and you have conquered every running challenge in the country. When it comes to running, you're a machine and you can just get it done. Well, what are you going to do next? You might set your sights on the Ironman challenge. Fantastic! Of course, in addition to running you're also going to have to bike and swim long distances as well. You're going to have to add bicycling and swimming into your daily training regimen, without neglecting you running through it all.

So, as you're catching your breath after stepping out of the Zone, take stock. What do you need to add, subtract, or just change in your business, schedule, or life to get to the next level?

Fight through the Good to Get to the Great

Top achievers aren't satisfied with getting to the Zone once or twice in a lifetime. They strive to get back there as often as they can. So should you. The more time you spend in the Zone, the more you accomplish and the more you learn about yourself. You want to push yourself to work harder and to get back there time and again.

As part of that, you have to realize that "good" isn't good enough. So many times, people get comfortable with good instead of pushing the envelope and striving for great. A lot of people are content to coast through life without ever seeing just how much better it could be if they were only willing to put forth the effort and try to reach beyond what they currently have, do, and are.

It's all about realizing that you are sufficing. A lot of people are afraid of trying because they don't want to fail. Take a moment, though, and instead of focusing on what you could lose, focus instead on what you could gain. It's all about feeding that restless part of you that in the quiet moments asks, "Is this all there is? Is this the best it gets?" That voice is telling you what you already know deep inside. There is more. There is better. You have to be willing to push forward to get it, not once in a while, not once in a lifetime, but every day.

"H" ZONE INTERVIEW ADVICE

from R. Anthony - Singer/Songwriter, TV Contestant on The Voice

> **"The highs and the lows, it adds to your development. It makes this combination of something great. If you never fail, you never experience the drive to get back up and do it. That drive pushes you to go beyond the limits."**
>
> **- R. Anthony**

Local Tampa Bay resident R Anthony took his singing talents to season three of the hit NBC TV show The Voice. His experience and journey was absolutely incredible. He made the cuts all the way to LA to perform his blind audition on TV, in front of a 15 million viewing audience and also in front of the four celebrity judges: Christina Aguilera, Blake Shelton, Adam Levine, and CeeLo. In an amazing turn of events both Christina and CeeLo wanted him on their team.

POWER TIP #9

DEVELOP A STRONG, CONSISTENT WORK ETHIC OF PRACTICE AND REPETITION

Perfect practice makes perfect.

The admission ticket that's required to get to peak performance, to get in the Zone, is an undeniably strong, consistent work ethic when it comes to practice and repetition. In order to master anything, you have to put in the time. There are no shortcuts. A lot of people cite 10,000 hours of intentional effort that's required to become an expert at something or master a skill. While that number can vary, the underlying principle is correct. You can't just decide to do something and become an expert overnight. You have to work at it consistently and practice, practice, practice. Even then, you need to be practicing the right thing in the right way.

Practice makes perfect, or so the saying goes. That's not entirely true. You see, I could practice and practice and do the same thing on the golf course with the ugliest golf swing, hour after hour, and all I'll do is perfect doing that swing wrong. It's not just practice, that's required. It's perfect practice that makes perfect.

This can be where it's helpful to hire coaches or find mentors who can help you. A golf pro can tell you exactly what you're doing wrong with your golf swing and help you change your stance and the way you're doing it so that you practice doing it the right way instead of the wrong way. In this way, you can save yourself thousands of hours of wasted practice doing something that won't be effective or get you the results you're looking for.

It's important to remember that there are no guarantees. Even if you put in the time, you might still fall short of the mark if you have no passion for what you're trying to master or lack some basic skills or requirements generally needed for the goal you're trying to attain. You might put in 10,000 hours on the football field, but you might lack some of the physical requirements such as size and speed to make it in the NFL. Remember that part of getting to the Zone is having realistic, attainable goals that challenge and stretch you.

No matter what you want to do in life, if it's important to you, then it's worth putting forth your best effort. If something isn't worth spending hundreds or even thousands of hours working at, then you need to rethink why you're trying to achieve that goal in the first place!

POWER TIP #10
THE POWER OF MANAGING YOURSELF

The greatest victory one can achieve is to conquer oneself.

As we just discussed, perfect practice and repetition are key to making it into the Zone. However, not everyone looks forward to putting in hours and hours of work, oftentimes without being able to see some kind of immediate, tangible reward for it. That's why self-discipline, the ability to control your emotions and keep yourself on task, is vital to getting into the Zone.

Some days, you show up to the office and you're just not in the mood. You don't want to have to prepare for presentations, you'd rather skip the meetings; you don't want to make calls. You don't even really want to be there at all. It's when you don't feel like it that you need the mental fortitude to force yourself to push forward. Nobody likes the grind, but you need to be able to force yourself through it, with focus, or inspiring words, or a stern lecture—whatever it takes. You do that knowing that you're going to come out better on the other side.

In the morning sometimes, I'd rather just sleep in instead of getting up and working out. It's awfully tempting. I know that working out will be good for me, though, and that if I don't start the day that way, it will throw everything off. So, how do I motivate myself when the bed is comfy and I'm tired? I've learned a couple of tricks.

In the first five seconds of the thought process, instead of dwelling on the decision, I force myself to physically move. I think to myself, "I need to do this. Let's make this happen." You see, the minute I let my mind start to contemplate sleeping in, I'm in trouble. So, I force action as quickly as possible. I do the same with other parts of my day, such as making that first phone call. I learned that from Mel Robbins.

The great thing is, once you start, you have momentum on your side. Suddenly, I'm halfway through that workout or I'm done with the first call and I'm on to the next. As the momentum begins to carry me through those tasks, I become grateful that I jumped on them and I really start to get into the groove.

You see, looking at the bridge you have to cross can be overwhelming, but if you force yourself to start walking, you've soon crossed it and things become easier. Then you start to feel the benefits. I feel healthy for working out and I start reflecting on how I want to be around for years and years and stay healthy for my family. The bigger picture comes into focus. At the end of the day, holding onto that bigger picture can get you through even when you're tired and ready to give up.

That momentum that you build up doesn't just carry you through the task at hand. It can carry you through the whole day if you let it. That's because everything is connected. In the morning, I work out and then I feel better. I shower and get suited up feeling even better and more confident about tackling the next things in my day because I've already had success tackling something right off. Now, I'm ready to go to work and I'm charged up. I'm ready to make phone calls, sell my ideas, pitch to a new company, or talk up a new product or service. New opportunities and training all come easier.

Insanity and craziness come from lack of organization and being spread out all over the place instead of being focused. You need to visualize.

You need to see where you want to end up. You need to see that clearly and play it like a mind movie. See it, and feel it, what it looks like and feels like. You want to lose twenty pounds for the New Year? What is it going to feel like to achieve that? You want to generate another $20,000 dollars of income? How will that feel and what will it enable you to do? You want to increase your business, learn a new skill, or anything else? It's all doable. First, you have to win that battle of getting up out of bed and getting going. You need to keep your eye on the prize.

Muhammad Ali, a man I admired, said that a prize fight is like a war. The real part of the war is won or lost somewhere far away from the witnesses, behind the lines, in the gym, and out there on the road long before he dances underneath the lights in the arena. So, what he's saying is that it's in the gym, it's preparing, it's doing war with himself long before he gets out there into the boxing ring and does battle with someone else that the battle is won or lost. When he steps into the ring, it's already decided. The real war is preparing to be in that arena. It's the same thing in business. The real war is keeping yourself focused and moving forward even when no one is looking.

POWER TIP #11
FOCUS ON THE LARGER PURPOSE
OF THE ACTIVITY

"We cannot hold a torch to light another's path
without brightening our own."
—Ben Sweetland

To help you stay focused and motivated the activity that you're doing needs to be tied to a larger purpose. That purpose helps you get through the day to day tasks and is necessary to help you plant the seeds to reach your peak performance in the Zone. Again, it's not just about the goal; it's about what the goal means.

Say I have ten phone calls I want to make today, and I don't feel like making them. Well, the ten calls are tied to a larger purpose, right? It's not just about the act of making the call and talking to someone. I have a larger purpose, a higher calling when it comes to those calls. I want to help people, somebody beyond myself and beyond my team. I want to help my clients. I think about them and the people I'm helping to empower. And by helping them, I help their businesses to be more successful and get to the next level. I'm helping businesses avoid failure, avoiding a downturn in the marketplace with their products and services. I'm helping businesses succeed, grow more jobs, create more opportunities, and offer their products and services with what I'm delivering. It's not just about helping me and my company, but about helping all those other companies and the people that work for them.

If I have a bigger picture, bigger purpose, that's going to be part of the service mindset that I have to keep me inspired, to keep me moving in the right direction of where I want to go. Without that, it's easy to lose your way.

Some people have trouble seeing the right picture, the right purpose, and holding on to it. Sometimes, they lose their faith in the purpose because they take their eyes off it and look around them. They see stacks of bills, failure all around them, naysayers telling them how hard it is to make it, the competition crushing it. Even when things are dark, it's imperative to keep moving forward because you're getting closer to your breakthrough. That larger purpose is what will help you stay the course when you're tired and discouraged.

STEPPING INTO YOUR
BUSINESS ZONE

"If you are not willing to risk the usual, you will settle for the ordinary."
—*Jim Rohn*

Seventy million people in America are employed by small businesses. There are roughly thirty million small businesses, 75% of which are owned and operated by a single person. Half of all small businesses operate out of the owner's home.

Anyone can be an entrepreneur. Oftentimes, owning a business provides opportunities that people struggle to get at other jobs. It doesn't matter who you are or where you come from, you can start up your own business. You don't have to have a lot of money. You don't have to have a product that is going to rocket you to billion-dollar Silicon Valley type success. It's easier than ever to get started with just a small idea.

There is tremendous opportunity now in all areas for everybody to be part of this new digital age, this new communication age, the new efficiency of resources to starting a business. You can find the connection to what you like. You can find the connection to what you have a passion for because this, right here, is a game-changer.

It's time for you to step into your business Zone. That business you've always wanted to start? Now's the time. That sales record you've always wanted to break? It's within your grasp. You just need to learn to push yourself to be your best.

CHAPTER 26

Media and Your Fan Base

Do something today that your future self will thank you for.

Technology moves fast. We all know it. We can watch it changing all around us. There are marketing strategies available to us today that didn't even exist a decade ago. The top achievers know that learning new skills and keeping up with the latest cutting-edge tools are essential to helping them grow and expand their businesses and themselves.

New Media

The old media is dying. The new media has taken over. One of the single, most powerful marketing tools ever put into the hands of businessmen and salespeople is the prevalence of social media. Facebook, Twitter, Instagram, LinkedIn, and half a dozen other sites allow you to connect instantly and directly with your clients and potential customers. It removes the barriers to communication and helps your satisfied customers become cheerleaders who spread the word about you across the country and even the globe.

It used to be that good word of mouth got you sales in a town, section of a city, or a particular industry. Now, you have access to a much wider pool of customers. The ability for people to share their experiences on review sites makes it that much more crucial that you stay on top of interacting with your clients.

The word of the day is "access." Everyone is looking for access to information about everything. The more time you spend on your website, on social media, on reviewing sites, the more access you're granting customers. They want your time, your attention, and your answers to their questions. They also want to see behind the veil and know more about the people and companies they do business with.

Print is dead. The real action is virtual and online these days. People want information and they love being able to research anything at a moment's notice. One of the challenges of standing out and capturing attention in the current marketplace is just the sheer amount of noise you have to be able to cut through. You need to be able to grab people's attention. The best way to do that is videos.

The Power of Videos

The power of video in today's market is second to none. As a serial entrepreneur, one of my companies that I've built over the last eighteen years is a video production media agency. The company's called "In The Zone TV."

Did you realize that the average person remembers only 20% from what they read and only retains 30% of what they hear? However, people are able to remember at an incredible 70% retention rate when it comes to videos. That's why successful companies use them to convert leads into sales. YouTube has over five billion videos viewed a day, and over thirty billion hours of video is watched each month. More videos are uploaded in one month than the three major TV networks combined created in sixty years. When you watch videos, you're able to visually process images 60,000 times faster than reading text. So, the digital evolution has just made it so much easier to reach and engage customers and clients.

Over 80% of people watch videos every week, and that's why social media is unlocking opportunities. If you're not using videos to express your company's purpose and passion, you're going to be left behind. Since 2003, I have successfully produced countless videos for clients, TV projects, websites, YouTube channels, and social media. Our award-winning production team provides cutting edge strategies to drive bottom line results. Today, video is a must-have marketing tool. People want to watch and not read.

Just having videos on your website can increase your rank on Google and search engines by 53%. Videos will increase your click ratio in an email. Audiences are ten times more likely to engage with you based on watching video content than reading three or four pages on your website. Videos are a quick way of introducing people to your product and your business while you have 100% control of your image. Instead of getting on the phone to try and talk for twenty minutes, wouldn't it be great to send a two-minute video to a prospect and say, "Hey, check me out. Here's who we are. Here's what we do." A good video will elicit emotions from the viewer. When you can inform and entertain people and trigger an emotional response in them it pushes people to engage.

When you're looking at profile videos for yourself or your company, you want to make sure they are well-produced. The video has to show you and highlight who you are, what you do, why you're compelling, and why people should engage with you. There are a few different styles of video to choose from.

Documentary Style: This style has no voiceover. You see the owner and/or employees on screen, talking about the company and the product. Oftentimes, there is high production value with music and edgy footage that's dynamic in nature.

Newsmercial: This video presents the information as though it's a news piece. The viewer is being informed of something. These can be incredibly effective because we're raised since childhood to receive information in the form of a newscast. Viewers often give the newsmercial a similar level of credibility. It also comes across as helpful instead of just "selling," which can hook people in more.

Credibility Endorsement: These are very highly produced videos with million dollar sets and top talent. They give your business or product a polished, professional look that lets people know this is a serious, top tier business.

Isolated Videos: These videos, also called micro videos, don't focus on the whole picture. Instead, they are companion pieces that just focus in on one thing. They might highlight one particular product. They can also be used to announce a holiday sale or something of that nature.

Testimonial Videos: You see these on television a lot. Someone who looks trustworthy tells you about their experience with the product so that you can feel good making a decision to buy it. Everyone wants to make a good decision and videos of people sharing their stories of success with the product or service promotes your brand three times more powerfully than you can. Think about it, there's a built-in belief that someone wouldn't endorse a product or service if they didn't believe in it. We cling to this belief even when we know that whoever's giving the testimonial was paid to do so. The viewer is putting their trust in the integrity of the person telling them that the product worked great for them.

FAQ Videos: Frequently Asked Questions (FAQ) videos can be an extremely powerful tool. How many times have you gotten tired of answering the same five questions that nearly every client seems to have? Worse, how many times have you found that a client didn't retain the information and so you have to answer the same question for the same client over and

Step Into Your Zone

over? It can be frustrating and a waste of everyone's time. Since videos provide a much higher retention rate of information than either the printed or spoken word do, it makes sense to help both yourself and your clients with use of this tool. You can have individual videos addressing each question. You can also cover the basics like videos on how to use the product or service.

Whether you have a long video, short video, self-made or professionally produced video, it's an excellent sales tool. It's like having a superstar salesperson as an asset, as an ally, as your teammate to get business. They are an investment, not a cost. A cost is money that's lost. When you invest a dollar and the video feeds you back $5 in new sales opportunities, that's an investment. Today, more than ever, you need videos to help you get more conversions, higher conversion, more opportunities, and build your brand because that video is working for you 24/7. You don't have to invest a fortune either. I've done videos for clients for as little as $1,000 to help them be successful and promote their brand and identity.

Video is how you take your game to the next level. You don't just stop with one, though. It's about having hundreds of videos out there working for you. They represent you, your business, and your brand in the marketplace. Each of them is working for you round the clock, creating awareness. That's crucial because the single biggest problem that small businesses have is they are dealing with obscurity. They need to establish their brand identity and fight through obscurity. You can do this through Facebook posts and Twitter ads, each of which can have a video. You need to create awareness. And, just like the journey to the Zone, it all starts with a single step. The goal is to have hundreds of videos out there in the world, but you just need to get the first one done to get yourself started.

With a wide variety of video marketing solutions, you can connect your message to the digital world that can help you stand out and get noticed. Take advantage of various video solutions that include:

newsmercials, profile videos, special events, TV coverage, commercials, testimonials, training videos, online interviews, and other turnkey branding solutions. Tell your story to the world so you can stand out and dramatically grow your business. What story do you want to share with the world?

"H" ZONE INTERVIEW ADVICE

from Darren Prince - Sports Agent, Writer, Speaker

> **"I started to [understand] it's the power of media, the power of surrounding yourself with people that know a lot more and really just leveraging these guys to elevate [your] brand."**
>
> **- Darren Prince**

Darren Prince is a legendary sports and entertainment agent who started his career as a kid when he built a multi-million dollar business selling baseball cards.

CHAPTER 27

Social Media Guide

*"The beauty of today's world is people can wake up in the morning, come up
with an idea and literally within days or weeks, take it on a global basis."*
—Kevin Harrington

Social media refers to sites and applications where people from across the
globe connect, communicate, interact, and share content with each other
in real time. These platforms provide an excellent way for customers, business owners, and brands to build and strengthen relationships. Through
these platforms you can share photos, opinions, feedback, and other information instantly. The massive outreach of social media channels is clearly
evident from the statistics, insights, user base, and usage data. It shows that
social media platforms such as LinkedIn, Facebook, Twitter, and Instagram
are not a fad but are here to stay. Therefore, every business owner should
include social media as part of their digital marketing plan and leverage all
the leading platforms to their business advantage.

In today's digital world, merely having a brick and mortar store or
a website is not enough to succeed. If you want to take your business to

greater heights, you must incorporate social media in your strategic mix and create accounts on different platforms to increase customer engagement and interaction. Let's just say social media is your best bet to stay relevant, connected, and competitive.

Top Benefits of Social Media for Businesses

Create Brand Recognition and Awareness: One of the most important marketing goals is to create brand recognition and awareness. This is important so that people recognize your brand instantly when you advertise it and connect with it. Brand recognition and awareness also help nurture a trust-based relationship with the audience and the brand. When they can trust your brand that is when they are most likely to give your business products or services a try and convert from prospects to customer. Social media allows for easy as well as effective brand building. Unlike old school methods of advertising, social media can get your business right in front of your audience easily and quickly. In order to improve brand awareness on social media platforms, here's what you can do:

1. Research top social media platforms to find out whether your target audience is on it. You can do this by searching for relevant conversations about your industry or product on it.

2. Once you do your legwork and get a good understanding of the platforms where your target audience is, then try to grab their attention by using creative visuals and content such as blogs, case studies, videos and more. Remember that videos and images play a crucial role in brand awareness. Videos not only increase user engagement but also help get more social shares.

3. Spark a conversation with your prospects. You can do this by responding to queries ASAP, conversing, tagging, and even mentioning others.

Faster and Easier Communication: Today, when everything is at our fingertips, customers expect businesses to respond to their queries, reservations, and feedback immediately. That is what you can ensure when you create a social media presence for your business. Social media allows your customer representative to receive, review, and respond to your customer questions and grievances fast and resolve them to their complete satisfaction. It truly allows brands to deliver award-winning customer service and retain customers.

Improved Customer Engagement: As communication is fast and you have a platform where you can post and upload videos, content, and information about your brand and share it with your audience, this promotes customer engagement. After all, who doesn't like quality content be it blogs or videos? Social media provides your brand the power to keep your audience hooked and engaged. The more you engage your customers, the more likely they are to talk about your brand and buy from you. In other words, customer engagement can lead to higher conversion rate and more sales thereby generating your business more profits.

Increased Web Traffic: Social media allows you to create a new channel, which is great for drawing laser targeted inbound traffic and getting more inbound links. For example, you have an active blog where you post fresh content. If you have a Facebook page or a Twitter account, you can increase your market outreach by ten times thus accessing a bigger audience that may like and even share your content.

How to Leverage Facebook for Social Media Marketing

Based on the results of your marketing efforts and target audience engagement, you should select the platforms to focus on the most. However, here is a general overview on how you can use the top social media platforms to ensure business performance, growth, and customer engagement. Let's start with the leading platform first...shall we?

With approximately 1.62 billion monthly active users and counting, 30 percent of which log in and spend roughly 20 minutes every day, Facebook is the most popular and rapidly growing social media communication channel that there is today. It is a massively effective platform for marketers and consumers alike.

According to a survey conducted by Hootsuite, 98% of business owners use Facebook for business marketing and 30% claim that Facebook offers the highest returns on investment of any social media platform.

Hence, the best way for marketers to leverage on Facebook for business success is to invest in Facebook advertising. Facebook advertising gives marketers the power and control to modify ads to suit their exact needs and targeted results. Therefore, through this advertising tool you can target audience by a variety of factors including but not limited to age, gender, employment, interests, relationship status, or purchasing behaviors.

This can be used as a major advantage as you can target your exact audience with precision by narrowing it down greatly. Thus, you can put your business ads and content in their newsfeed thereby ensuring that your message gets right in front of your audience. It's practically impossible to miss or ignore.

Moreover, the broad appeal of Facebook gives you the perfect chance to convert your customer base into a community. On Facebook, you can create your own business page and start posting interactive and informational content to keep your customers and followers informed and up to date and direct them to your website.

However, there's perhaps one obvious instance where you may have to choose another platform for business promotion if Facebook prohibits ads of your company based on its ad policies. For example, if you have a tobacco or vaping company, then you may not be allowed to advertise on Facebook.

Here are some steps to get you started:

— Decide on your campaign goal.
— Choose the right ad format as per your needs, audience and goal and optimize it in numerous ways like traffic, engagement, leads, and purchase objectives. Some popular ad formats include video ads, canvas ads, photo ads, slideshow ads and augmented reality ads. For example, slideshow ads are excellent for highlighting and displaying product lines.
— Create your offer.
— Set the target audience and budget. Facebook allows you to create lookalike and custom audiences so you can precisely target your demographic.

How to Increase Followers on Facebook

Some of the best tips to increase followers on Facebook are

— Advertise on Facebook
— Invite people to your page and like it
— Create shareable and viral content
— Host giveaways
— Stir reader engagement with interesting content
— Use Facebook Live (this is live streaming). The more viewers that you have on your live stream, the higher you will appear on the feed.

— Using Influencer Marketing on Facebook. Brands are now collaborating actively with influencers across channels to tap the power of social media and the impact that influencers have on their followers to generate brand awareness, create a strong brand perception, and generate leads. As more than 80% of consumers trust word of mouth recommendations, just imagine what influencers can do for your business. Try sharing influencer content on your Facebook to stir customer engagement.

How to Leverage Twitter for Social Media Marketing

Most known for its real-time and concise updates and tweets, Twitter is one of the most popular social media platforms for businesses to create buzz and keep audiences engaged. People, on the other hand, love Twitter because it gives them a steady stream of new content and information practically all the time. Therefore, it is not surprising to see men and women of all ages on Twitter. The average number of monthly users on Twitter is 330 million.

Most certainly your business has the opportunity to reach millions and likewise, grow tremendously. Hence, to tap this platform your brand should be active on Twitter. Try to send out a tweet every now and then. Since Twitter limits its users to messages of 280 characters, you don't have to do much. Informative and interesting tweets will do the job and keep people tweeting about your business. And that is what you want to increase brand awareness and customer engagement. This can get you re-tweets thereby reaching out to a broader audience.

Twitter Advertising

According to the latest research by Twitter, this social media platform offers a 50% year on year increase in advertisement engagement which is coupled with a 14% year-on-year decline in cost/engagement. You can sponsor accounts, tweets, or trends to advertise on Twitter. Promoted tweets are equal to Instagram ads. Although they look similar to regular tweets, they feature a small promoted label that signify their ad status. Moreover, promoted accounts enable you to advertise your account to your audience who don't follow you already.

Likewise, promoted trends allow your brand to promote a hashtag featuring in the trending section. Therefore, when people click on the trend, they will get to see the promoted tweet at the top of the list of results. These three types of Twitter ads really make it easy for businesses to use Twitter and get people talking about their brand.

Here are the steps to advertise on Twitter:

— Step up your Twitter ad account
— Choose your goal
— Set up the ad group and bid. You can either control the bid manually or let it work automatically. It is all up to you. If you choose automatic bidding, then Twitter will automatically set your bid helping you get the best results at the lowest prices according to your budget. However, if you choose to go manual then the Twitter interface will show you bids based on what others are paying so that you can bid smartly.
— Choose your ad placement
— Select target audience
— Launch campaign

How to Leverage Instagram for Social Media Marketing

Instagram has more than 1 billion monthly users. Hence, brands across industries actively look for ways to interact with the Instagram community and attract their customers so that they keep coming back for more. According to Instagram, 60% of users say they discover new products on the platform and 75% of Instagrammers take action after being inspired by a post.

People on Instagram are shoppers. That means that if you post the right images, your prospects will understand and soak up your brand message without the hard sales pitch from you. So, with the right pictures you can attract, appeal to, and convert customers without selling to them. Isn't that interesting? However, make sure that the photos are professional, top quality, and creative. Here are some of the best tips to leverage Instagram for business growth and success:

— Studies show that brighter and lighter images generate 24% more likes as compared to images that are dark.
— Create unique lifestyle photos that capture brand culture for customer engagement.
— Don't forget to offer promotions as well as exclusive announcements to followers.
— Instagram is ideal for companies operating in digital tech and fashion industries in comparison to those focused on home building and agriculture. This is because it has a bigger following in urban areas. Young and trendy companies are more likely to be successful on Instagram and experience greater growth in their business.

Instagram Advertising

Tap the power of Instagram advertising for business growth and promotion. These ads are native thus they appear through the customer feed naturally. So, it allows you to advertise without being salesy. Besides this, advertising on Instagram is sleek, seamless, and simple.

Here's how to set up ads on Instagram:

— Navigate to your ad manager within Facebook. Keep in mind that there is no ad manager on Instagram. As Instagram is owned by Facebook, you will have to use Facebook ad manager to manage ads on Instagram.

— Choose your campaign goal. Such as do you need more traffic, video views, or increase brand awareness. Please note that Instagram ads work only with the following goals: reach, brand awareness, traffic, app installs, post engagement, video views, and website/app conversions.

— Configure your target audience. This is needed to ensure that you target your appropriate audience and get your ad listed in front of the right people. Configure your ads using factors such as location, age, demographics, gender, languages, interests, behaviors, connections, custom audience, and lookalike audience.

— Choose your ad placement. Here it is important to note that you must choose and edit placements tab especially if you have created content exclusively for Instagram. This is because if you don't do that then, Facebook will automatically show it on both platforms (Facebook and Instagram).

— Decide on the schedule of your advertisement on Instagram and set your budget accordingly. As your campaign runs on Instagram, you can pause and control it any time that you want, especially if you think that the budget is not allocated properly and you need to adjust it for better results or cost control or whatever the reason may be. A great tip here is that you can optimize your budget by running the ad schedule smartly. Do your share of the legwork to target specific times of day and days of the week when you know that your audience is most active on Instagram.

How to Increase Instagram Followers

In order to increase your followers on Instagram, try to interact with the content of other people. It is a great method of getting followers. Also, reposting content such as stories and posts work like a magnet when it comes to increasing followers.

Besides this, studies show that people like to get attention from brands, so if your brand interacts with them, it is likely to increase your follower count.

In addition to this, hashtags are also an effective way to up your followers on Instagram. However, to get the best results, the trick is to use a lot of niche specific hashtags. Try using up to 30 hashtags per post. This will help attract your target audience. In other words, don't opt for general hashtags, try to be specific. Use hashtags that align with your page and tells the audience what it's about.

How to Leverage LinkedIn for Social Media Marketing

This platform is perfect if your target audience is professionals. This is where professionals connect and network. LinkedIn allows businesses to target audience based on their professions.

LinkedIn advertising has numerous unique advantages that put it in a class of its own. Some of the top benefits of using LinkedIn apart from reaching a more professional audience include the following:

— Allows you to narrow your targeting using industry specific variables like job titles, functions, seniority, industry, skills, and degree type
— Gives you the power to choose from a variety of advertising formats empowering you to target messages to niche audiences
— Helps you leverage on lead nurturing possibilities
— Increase your conversion rate

According to a study by HubSpot, they found out that LinkedIn ads have the potential to convert users to leads at a 6.1% conversion rate.

All this shows that LinkedIn is a powerful medium and if used the right way, it has the potential to deliver marketers amazing success.

LinkedIn Advertising

Here are the steps to start advertising on LinkedIn the right way:

— Build brand persona. To do this, create a list of your ideal customer key traits as well as demographic information.
— Narrow down you customer persona by using options like job experience, company name, interests, and education. All this will allow you to describe your target customer on LinkedIn thus helping you get your message in front of the right people.
— Choose the ad type on LinkedIn. In general, there are three formats—sponsored content, text ads, and message ads. Sponsored ads have the potential to earn approximately 400–500% leads. These ads appear directly in your target audience LinkedIn feed. It refers to the content that you sponsor. For the success of these ads, you must ensure that you run sponsored ads that convert leads upon prospect content engagement. Text ads appear around the web pages that are viewed by your audience while they are on LinkedIn. For these ads, you can test different variations. Use the power of split testing to create a result-focused advertisement. Message ads are different from sponsored and text ads. By using LinkedIn messenger, they help deliver personalized content. These ads are bought on a cost/send basis; thus, you only pay for the messages that get delivered on desktop and mobile.
— Once you choose your ad format, optimize your campaign by using A/B testing. This will help you get the best results.

Some tips to get best results include the following:

— Change only a few criteria at a time. In other words, isolate the part of your test that impacts performance such as test job skills vs. titles or function vs. industry.

— Change around your landing pages or experiment with contacting people who sign up with you to see if they can be converted into customers on call as opposed to using an auto responder for converting them.

— Run new ads on a monthly basis to avoid banner blindness. Banner blindness occurs when your audience becomes used to watching the same ads and become less responsive toward them. Therefore, new ads are important to stir engagement and keep them hooked.

Tracking and Measuring Your Social Media Campaigns

Once you choose the right social media platforms for your business and start advertising on them, it's important that you simultaneously track, monitor, and measure the performance of your social media ads and campaign.

This will help you determine if the ad results conform to your expectations. Moreover, you'll be able to see if your campaign is working successfully toward achieving your targeted goals. If the results or performance of the campaign are not aligned with your targeted goals, you can make changes accordingly and focus on the areas of improvement.

The best way to track and measure campaigns on social media is to use tools like Google Analytics and Social Report. You can also use the built-in analytics on every social media. These are easy to use and quite effective. All this will help you understand exactly how effective your social media campaigns are and how to improve them for even better results.

To stay relevant and ensure business growth and success, you must include social media in your digital marketing plan. Advertising on social media can help get your business noticed, create brand awareness, and keep your audience engaged.

"H" Zone Interview Advice

from Darren Prince - Sports Agent, Writer, Speaker

"...within like a few weeks after signing Magic Johnson, I remember my dad humbled me... I hired a publicist and yeah, just like that. I was in [a] Page Six article -Super Agent Darren Prince signs Magic Johnson. I bring the paper home, there was no internet back then. My dad...says, let me explain something to you. You're not the super agent. Magic is Superman. That's why they're calling you that. Yeah, so I started to really understanding that it's the power of media, the power of surrounding yourself with people that know a lot more and really just leveraging these guys to elevate our brand." - Darren Prince

Darren Prince is a legendary sports and entertainment agent who started his career as a kid when he built a multi-million dollar business selling baseball cards.

CHAPTER 28

Marketing Your Team and Personal Brands

"Help others achieve their dreams and you will achieve yours."
—Les Brown

In the digital information age, when there is a global community and access to information and services 24/7 you need to find ways to stand out. You have to be on your game when it comes to marketing. Differentiating yourself from the competition is the key. You can do that through added value and solid branding.

Incentive Marketing

Staying one step ahead of the competition can be hard. You can't always do so by offering the best price, but you can also offer great service and other perks.

Big companies can come in and undercut the market. They can afford to bleed money for a year or two while they drive all their competitors out. You can't undervalue the product or service you offer because that will hurt you and ultimately kill your company. You have to maintain the value of integrity in the pricing. So, what you do to compete is add value to the deal to create differentiation.

How do you add value? There are a number of ways. You can offer a Buy One Get One at 50% incentive. You can offer loyalty programs or gift incentives. What I've found the most effective, though, is when you add a compelling, exciting, experiential trip incentive experience for the customer. This fulfills a customer's need to be recognized and appreciated. It's a strong human motivator which brings the fun and creates more viral marketing for the company.

Everybody is looking for the experiential these days. Travel is one of the best ways to give it to them. This type of incentive works particularly well if you're selling business to business where the company buying from you could spend anywhere from twenty thousand to two million on your product, service, or solution. There are two real types of travel incentives: group and individual.

Group travel is when a customer buys a certain volume from you and then you take them on a trip with all your other customers who meet the criteria. These trips can be a lot of fun, but there are limitations.

First, when you're paying to bring your customer, distributor, or contractor and their spouse, you're spending five thousand and up for them. That means you can only afford to offer this incentive for your very top tier customers. You can't afford to do that for your mid-level customers. You're not motivating your entire customer base.

Second, when you offer the experience to a whole group of people, you're not able to give one-on-one attention to everyone. There might not be an opportunity and your customer may want to be with their spouse doing their own thing.

241

Third, not everyone's schedules will match up. Your top client might not be able to come because it's the same week as their daughter's wedding, for example, and so they send their assistant instead. That's great for the assistant, but not for you. The top-tier customer might even demand that you do something separate for them since they can't go.

Individual travel incentive packages offer the best, most flexible solution. It appeals to big customers and small customers alike. As it is individual, they choose when they go, who they go with, and sometimes even where they go. You also have the opportunity to tier the experience based on the amount of business you do with them. As the customers hit different levels of growth or sales then they get different types of travel experiences. It's the treadmill effect. When they start, they hit level one, they hit level two, they hit level three. The more they buy from you, the more they qualify for. It creates a whole opportunity for businesses to increase their loyalty and increase the new business opportunities for you. Generally, I like having an eight-tier program.

A tier one experience would be a drive-away weekend, which covers hotel, gas money, and golfing, which costs about $500. As the tiers progress the vacations get nicer and more expensive. A tier three experience could be a national flyaway including hotel and roundtrip airfare for two in the domestic United States. That tier costs around $1,850. A level six tier might be an Alaskan cruise. A level eight tier could be a Superbowl or Masters Golf package.

The great thing about this is that you get to incentivize customers at every level. You're encouraging them to do business with you, give you their loyalty. This provides differentiation in the marketplace. You can sell based on added value experience. You can customize further so that you can either create the tiers based on sales levels, the actual amount they spend with you, or incremental growth targets where you reward customers based on their growth over last year. This encourages customers to spend more with you this year than they did last year.

When you have repeat customers who year after year do the same amount of business with you, there's a temptation to take them for granted and think that you don't want to spend money on an incentive for them because it's guaranteed business. What I say is there's nothing guaranteed. Your competition would love to grab that customer from you. An incentive can work like an insurance policy in that regard, making sure that you've sweetened the pot and shown appreciation for that customer.

Of course, as a business owner, it's a good idea to reward both your customers and your sales force. Your sales force is crucial to getting new customers as well as retaining the old ones. Obviously, it's more comfortable for your sales team to deal with the existing customers instead of cold calling and pounding the pavement to find new ones. However, for any business to be healthy you need new customers as well as old ones. It's imperative that you have both.

Business Brand Versus Personal Brand

We talked about properly marketing because it doesn't matter what your product, your service, or even how great you are, if you don't market. If you cannot get people's attention to make them aware of what you have to offer, you can't even engage in the sales process. The reason most businesses don't succeed is because they don't market. It's imperative to market effectively, and it's also important to use marketing support collateral materials.

In today's marketing world, you need to have an efficient marketing strategy. Building a recognizable brand that people can trust is the key. When people need something, and they find over a hundred companies selling that item, reputation can play a huge role in whom they go with. Corporate branding is vital, but as a sales professional, you also need to define who you are and build your brand.

You need to work on your image and your reputation. Testimonial videos help greatly in this area. Potential customers can see what others who have taken advantage of your product or service have experienced throughout the process. A company can have a fantastic reputation but at the end of the day a bad salesman can send even longtime customers scurrying elsewhere.

There are three basic reasons people don't buy: no need, no money, and no trust. If people don't see or can't be convinced of their need for something, they won't buy. If they don't have the money or they don't see the value in what you're offering, they won't buy. The final reason someone won't buy is because they don't trust you. When you're able to use testimonials to reduce the perceived risk then you make it easier for people to buy from you. When you combine that with value added incentives, whether it's a gift card, a logo item, a free report, or an incentive trip it can help push people over the edge from potential customer to customer.

"H" Zone Interview Advice

from Kevin Harrington - Creator of the Infomercial, original shark on *Shark Tank*.

> **"I would go into the neighborhood, get one job done almost for free, just to cover the cost of my material. I take a picture before I did the job, I take a picture after then put a sign up across the driveway and I now had the before and after magical transformation... Little did I know, but this was setting me up for the wonderful world of infomercials later, which was all about the before and after and the magical transformation."**
>
> **- Kevin Harrington**

Kevin Harrington, an original "shark" on the hit TV show Shark Tank, is the creator of the infomercial and pioneer of the As Seen on TV brand. His work behind-the-scenes of business ventures has produced over $5 billion in global sales.

CHAPTER 29

The Game of Sales

"I've missed more than 9,000 shots in my career. I've lost almost 300 games. 26 times, I've been trusted to take the game winning shot and missed. I've failed over and over and over again in my life. And that is why I succeed."
—*Michael Jordan*

Chances are I'm not telling you anything you haven't already heard before. That's fine. You can ignore what I have to say, but the really high-performance achiever is going to stop and think about how they are applying these ideas I'm sharing to their day-to-day world. There's no magic formula, but there's a great foundation of practical advice that I've extracted from my experiences being part of start-up companies, building a marketing agency, being an athlete, doing production, and TV interviews, and being able to interact with successful people including billionaires. So, take what you can from all of this. Even if there's only one or two pieces of advice that help you stretch yourself or advance to the next level, then it's all worth it.

The key ability that is important to everyone in the business game— and in the life that we live—is the ability to communicate. You need to be able to persuade and sell your idea or concept. I don't care if you're an entrepreneur, a salesperson, an account executive, or a parent trying to communicate with your child trying to sell them on a concept or to counteract what they're trying to pitch you. The most important skill we can have is the ability to effectively persuade.

Every day, we are so blessed, we should wake up thankful that we're in the game of sales and that we're able to go out and make an impact, add value, offer a product, offer a service that can make a difference to somebody and that our income potential is unlimited. We can basically write our own check, create our own destiny, or create our own lifestyle in the game of sales. You want to go make a million dollars? Just go help somebody make 10 million dollars and you're going to make a million dollars. That concept in sales is really the foundation of having that passion and excitement to be in the world of sales and that's why I want to start with that concept as I get into the breakthrough strategies with you. When you're chasing the money, that's the hard way to make a living.

Product Representation or Product Service Representation

Those of us in the game of sales commit basically a third of our lives to this. Consistently, when I've interviewed high achievers, high performers whether they be actors, athletes, or billionaire businesspeople, they all have a passion for what they're doing. If you're not passionate about your product or service, if you're not committed to it, if you don't have that same belief about it as you did five years ago, you have a problem. You need to make a change and find a product or service that is congruent with what you believe in, congruent with your personality, because you need to have 100% of your entire being committed to that product. After all, you're going to be spending a third of your life selling it.

When you're passionate about something the pure energy of your belief and the strength of your commitment are conveyed in your voice and your body language. That's what moves people and you can't summon that kind of emotion about something you only like but don't love. You have to align yourself with the product or service that you love.

When you love it, time moves fast. I've spent seven hours on a red carpet waiting to get a two-minute interview. I've spent days in an editing room, non-stop, to meet a deadline for a presentation. Finding the thing you can sell that you are passionate about is 60% of the challenge. Find something you can be cheering like crazy for. If you're embarrassed, and don't believe in your product or services, you need to make a change because congruency will not be there with you. Follow your passion and the money will come.

It is Imperative that You Have Compelling Goals

Helen Keller said, "The only thing worse than being blind is having sight but no vision." Sometimes in life, we get into our day to day struggles and we lose our passion, our vision, our excitement about what the possibilities are. It's important in the game of sales that we create our opportunities. We can create so many ways to help people and sales is a vehicle to be more productive in helping people while being rewarded financially. The key thing is you need to have a vision of where you're headed to keep you fueled during the times of adversity.

You need to write your goals down. I suggest physically writing them down on paper instead of typing them into the computer. Your goals need to be compelling. It's key to state them as if they've already been attained. Start with your desired outcome and paint the picture for yourself as if you've already achieved the goal. For example, let's say your goal is to build a multi-million dollar business, and have twenty-five employees working for you. You need to focus on the end vision of what you see. Attach pictures, images, and raw emotion to that vision of what you need to accomplish. Start with the end vision and work backward, letting the progression guide you to your goals, and the things that you'll need to do to make that vision come true.

A lot of people like to take physical images and make vision boards or paste them into their journal. Some make cue cards with their goals on it that they review three times a day. Whatever works best for you do it. You need to give your subconscious a clear idea of where you are going then it will help you figure out the route to take to get there. You've got to own this process. When you're doing goal setting, think about what you would try to accomplish if you knew you couldn't fail.

It's surprising how many times people struggle with writing down what they actually want, what they aspire to. They'll feel guilt, in writing down their goals or they won't write something down because they think they can't do it, that it's unattainable. Right away, these people are cutting themselves off from opportunity. It's not for anyone, including you, to say that your dreams are too big or unworthy. If you find yourself struggling with guilt, doubt, or self-defeating thoughts, I have something for you to try. Set a timer for sixty seconds. When you hit start, immediately write down everything you aspire to and everything you want to accomplish in your lifetime. When the alarm sounds, stop writing. You might be surprised at how in just that short period of time you can see a pattern shaping up that reflects what you truly want. That's because the ticking clock which forced you to hurry also kept you from second-guessing and questioning everything you wrote down.

A little over twenty years ago, I was going through some really challenging times. I was in a very bad place. I sat on a park bench in the early morning. I had a pen and notepad. I decided to figure out my life, decided what I wanted my future to be. The very first thing I wrote on the paper was, "I assume responsibility." I got really honest with myself. I wrote down exactly what my current situation was and owned the fact that it was because of my actions or lack of actions. I then spent three hours going through goal setting. Fifteen years later, I found that piece of paper and discovered that most of the goals I had achieved in that time. At the time I'd written them down, many of them seemed impossible, and yet I still accomplished them. When you give your mind a clear vision with strong emotions attached, it finds a way to work to get you there.

Skill Development

Every high-performance athlete and businessman is geared toward self-improvement. We need to constantly be honing our skills and acquiring new ones. Between all the books, workshops, online courses, and instructional videos available to us online these days, there's no excuse to not hone a particular skill. We have endless information and we should always be taking the time to learn more, absorb knowledge, and increase our skill set.

The competition is always learning, always innovating, and is more than happy to take your current and prospective customers from you. You need to continue to educate yourself and acquire new skills to remain relevant in the marketplace. Not only will it allow you to sell better, it will also allow you to provide your customers with more service. It can even give you the leg up to create a new product or business stream.

When the economy slowed down, Nick Friedman and his partner knew that they had to do something new. College Hunks Hauling Junk had been very successful, but circumstances in the marketplace changed and not as many people were willing to pay for someone to haul away their junk. That's when they innovated and expanded. They built upon their existing skill set and created a new product: moving services. That move helped them continue to grow their company in a tough economy and now College Hunks Hauling Junk & Moving is a big name in the industry.

The added bonus of gaining new skills and information is that it helps give you more of a positive mindset. You'll feel more confident in your own abilities. Plus, if you listen to motivational talks it will help get you in a positive mindset. Focusing on the fact that you can achieve is half the battle. Remember, in the Zone, there is no room for self-doubt, and you have to believe that you can achieve exactly what you've set out to do.

You Have to Play the Numbers

You can have a vision and the skills, but if you don't play the numbers, none of the rest matters. I've trained and mentored hundreds of salespeople over the years and worked with companies around the country to inspire their teams to high levels of performance. No matter who you are, no matter what you're selling, you have to make the calls and give the pitches. You won't sell every single person you pitch, so you need to pitch a lot of them.

It's like in baseball. A top-level player can hit fifty homeruns in a season. However, that doesn't mean that they can only be up to bat fifty times. You can't expect them to hit a homerun every time. That baseball player needs about 500 plus at bats per season to get those 50 homeruns.

In the game of sales if you're not out there with activity, if you're not out there making sales calls, making presentations, giving people the opportunity to buy, then you can't be a high achiever. You also need to monitor and know your numbers. High performance achievers know how many appointments they're seeing every week. They know how many appointments they're converting every week. They know what their close ratio is and that's the foundation. The great Michael Jordan kept track of how he did in his storied basketball career. He's said, "I've missed more than 9,000 shots in my career. I've lost almost 300 games. 26 times, I've been trusted to take the game winning shot and missed. I've failed over and over and over again in my life. And that is why I succeed." It's all about taking the shot because you'll miss 100% of the shots you never take.

Imagine there was a reality TV show based on the most successful salesperson, and that reality show followed you around from morning until evening in your day to day job. What would that show look like? You wouldn't be content with getting two appointments in a week. You'd want to keep the numbers and activity high.

There will be a lot of rejections, but you need to grow a bit of a thick skin. Don't ignore them but take those rejections and figure out how you can do better. Maybe you can work on your timing or the execution of your pitch. You need to watch your numbers and learn what your average close is. Of course, you work on improving that, but you need to at least know what your minimum requirement is to operate at a certain level of sales.

Have Fun in the Process

You spend a third of your life on your career, you need to make it fun for yourself. You can't struggle your way to joy. High achievers don't just enjoy the actual sale, they enjoy all of it. They enjoy the prospecting, the referral, the networking, the presentation, and the customer service. It's not just about being the top sales performer of the year because that's a fleeting moment. It's about enjoying the process and the journey day in and day out and having a passion for what you do.

Also, other people enjoy spending time with people who are having fun and are more likely to be comfortable around you and want to interact and do business with you. You can spread joy which is contagious. When you have fun, the success will follow.

"H" Zone Interview Advice

from Kevin Harrington - Creator of the Infomercial, original shark on *Shark Tank*.

"Here I am, Mr Infomercial... and people are running away from watching television. There's been over 60 million people who've cut the cord from cable television just in the United States... I said I needed to find a new way because we saw sales declining. So, we started a digital division. We said, okay, maybe TV sales are dropping, but digital sales started surging. Now as a company, we do 80% of our business in the digital world. We had to make a shift."

- Kevin Harrington

Kevin Harrington, an original "shark" on the hit TV show Shark Tank, is the creator of the infomercial and pioneer of the As Seen on TV brand. His work behind-the-scenes of business ventures has produced over $5 billion in global sales.

CHAPTER 30

Stay in the Zone Mindset

Don't count the days that you're working. Make
the days that you're working count!

Now more than ever you've got to get in and stay in the Zone mindset. No one is going to hand you your dreams on a silver platter. The good news is there's never been a better time to get out there and make your dreams come true. The power is in your hands in a way it never has been before.

The downside is that once you get there, you've got to work to stay there. There are a thousand other people coming up behind you, who are willing to step up if you are tired or bored or just can't motivate yourself to stay at the top of your game.

It's not the mountain ahead of you. It's not the inspiration of the climb that's going to wear you out. It's not the mountain of obstacles that's going to wear you out. It's going to be that little, nagging pebble in your shoe that's going to prevent you from achieving and escalating up toward your climb toward success. The moment you let that get to you, you're going to veer off the path.

Make sure to take time every few weeks to recharge and reevaluate your plan. Check in with yourself to see how you're doing, what's working, what's not working, and what you need in order to continue moving forward.

It's important to cultivate a desire to read, grow, and learn throughout your life. Reinvent that childhood wonder and curiosity that growing up may have beat out of you. It's our ability to dream, to think outside the box, and to reach beyond what we think we are capable of that takes us to the next level in business and in life. With focus, preparation, and passion we can work to achieve Zone level performance in every area of our lives. Wishing you Gods blessings!

Matthew 17:20–"Our faith can move mountains."

RESOURCES

Visit my website or email me, and let's connect.

Website: HJohnMejia.com

Email: info@HJohnMejia.com

Let's talk about growing your business together:

— Private Business Consulting Sessions
— Media Training
— Sales Training
— Keynote Speeches
— Online Consulting
— Get the "H" Playbook for Business Growth
— Incentive Marketing Promotions
— Customer Loyalty Programs
— Trip Incentives
— Sales Promotions
— Sales Growth Programs
— Video and Media Marketing
— Television Production
— Podcast Interviews

More resources from my interviewees:

Kevin Harrington
KevinHarrington.TV

Nick Friedman
CollegeHunksHaulingJunk.com

Darren Prince
Get his best-selling book, *Aiming High*, on Amazon.
PrinceMarketingGroup.com

Follow R Anthony on Instagram
@ranthonymusic

Steve and Julie Weintraub
HandsAcrosstheBay.org
GoldandDiamondSource.com

Follow Kato Kaelin on Instagram
@Kato_Kaelin

Rhonda Shear
RhondaShear.com
RhondaShearSocialHour.com

Darryl Strawberry
FindingYourWay.com

ABOUT THE AUTHOR

Entrepreneur "H" John Mejia is an award-winning TV Host and Producer who has appeared on national, regional, and local television. During the course of his career, he has interviewed hundreds of celebrities, athletes, and TV personalities. His project/client portfolio represents top brands and names. His TV interviews have included Kim Kardashian, Kris Jenner, Ashton Kutcher, Warren Moon, Demi Moore, Evander Holyfield, Angelo Dundee, Jeb Bush, General Norman Schwarzkopf, Kevin Harrington, Kendra Wilkerson, P Diddy Combs, Deion Sanders, Tim Tebow, Marcus Allen, Titus O'Neil, Jose Canseco, and Darryl Strawberry among many others.

He has been part of growing several multi-million dollar companies and his client roster includes many Fortune 500, medium and small size businesses. His media, marketing, and sales expertise delivers his clients increased results and his creative campaigns help them stand out from the competition. He has worked with top brands, such as Procter & Gamble, Pepsi, Fox Sports, GM, Playboy Celebrity Golf, Trane, Charter Spectrum, Frito Lay, LeBron James Family Foundation, Super Bowl Parties, NAPA, Coca Cola, and Pepperidge Farm.

As a former College All-American football player (AP Honorable Mention, CoSIDA Academic All-American, and All-ECAC), he still remains one of his schools' (Towson University) all-time leading TE receivers in Receptions, Yardage, and Touchdowns scored. He did sign NFL, USFL, and MLFS free agent contracts after college. Today, "H" always brings his "A" game to the clients he serves. As a powerful speaker, his motivational talks and strategies have inspired thousands of people over the years with winning strategies to help them drive results and dominate the marketplace.

Born and raised in NYC (Jamaica, Queens), he graduated from Bayside H.S. He is first-generation born in America, both of whose parents were foreign immigrants (mother from Latvia and father from Colombia) who came to the US to seek freedom and opportunities. His life journey has also been filled with ups and downs. From struggles with self- sabotage, anxiety, to having feelings of not being good enough, especially when he was cut from the NFL. "H" constantly has evolved and found the road to inner peace and happiness, while learning the key strategies to spend more time in the 'Zone'. He feels we are all God's work in progress.

He currently lives in the Tampa Bay area with his wife and has two amazing daughters and stepson.